BEYOND YOUR CONFINES

The Key to Free Your Mind

**

Chris Warren-Dickins LLB MA LPC

A Zero Labels Book

All people described in this book are fictional for illustrative purposes only. No name, characteristic, or similarity should be taken as a reference to any actual person, living or dead.

Disclaimer: The contents of this book are for informational and supportive purposes only and are not intended to replace the services of a mental health or medical professional. Should you have any questions about the material set out in this book, contact your clinician or doctor. If you need immediate help and you are in crisis, seek immediate, professional help. Here are your options: Call 911 (if it is available in your area), take yourself to the emergency room of your nearest hospital, call a friend or family member, and ask them to take you to the nearest emergency room, call the National Suicide Helpline on 988 or https://988lifeline.org/

Beyond Your Confines
The Key to Free Your Mind

Print ISBN: 979-8-9851024-3-7 (Hardback)
Print ISBN: 979-8-9851024-2-0 (Paperback)

Printed in the United States of America
First printing edition 2022
Published by Zero Labels LLC
143 E Ridgewood Ave, #1484, Ridgewood, NJ 07450

Cover design by Anabeth Bostrup
Images in cover photo used under license from Shutterstock.com
Editing by Sophia Dembling
Headshot photo of Chris Warren-Dickins by Jean Terman Photography

PRAISE FOR *BEYOND YOUR CONFINES*

"This book is not only timely but critical reading for anyone looking for greater understanding of themselves and the unique and challenging times we are in. Chris's keen insights and focus on interconnectivity have provided a basis to begin healing through our own well-being and healthier relationships. This is indeed a roadmap to freedom.'"

- Dr Pamela Brodie

“If anyone still feels trapped since the pandemic began, *Beyond Your Confines* is certainly a key to free your mind. Chris Warren-Dickins adopts a novel approach to challenges to our mental health, and threads together the most pressing societal issues of our time.

But don’t just read *Beyond Your Confines.* As Chris encourages their readers to do, use this book to strike up a dialogue with others about how we can use our inner resources and wisdom to heal ourselves, each other, and the planet that we are living in. Reach *Beyond Your Confines* today.”

- Monty Moncrieff MBE

LEARN MORE

To learn more about this book, and others I have written, use the following link to receive updates:

http://eepurl.com/gD41jr

DEDICATION

For Julie Arliss and Nadia O'Connor,
who each helped me reach beyond the confines of my mind.
Without their help, I would never have found the world of
love that is Mike and my two daughters, Lucille and Willow.

Contents

AUTHOR'S NOTE

Terminology

As you make your way through *Beyond Your Confines*, you may find that my use of labels does not quite reflect your own experience, or even inadvertently offends you by failing to be inclusive. I have made every effort to avoid this, but if this happens, please let me know via the contact page on my website, www.chriswarrendickins.com

If You Are in Crisis

If you are in crisis, you must seek immediate, professional help. Here are some of the ways you can seek help. I will repeat these in Appendix Crisis, set out at the end of this book:

- Call 911 (if it is available in your area).
- Take yourself to the emergency room of your nearest hospital.
- Call a friend or family member and ask them to take you to the nearest emergency room.
- Call the National Suicide Helpline on 988 or https://988lifeline.org/

Know that when you are in crisis, your brain is less likely to function optimally. This means that you might only consider a limited list of options when there might be more ways to resolve the problems you are experiencing. For this reason, you should seek help so a trained professional can ensure your safety and help you get out of your current state of crisis.

INTRODUCTION

We are all jailors in a prison of our own creation.

Sebastian Jones peered out from his apartment and flinched when he saw the children playing ball on the street below. He could remember a time when life was that simple, and it cut him deeply to know that such innocence was lost beyond his reach. He could almost taste it on his lips, the salty air of free summers at the shore, and the indulgence of sugary treats that tasted so much better when shared. Those days before the bills, before the career prospects (or lack of them), and before the in-fighting at work and within his family. And no matter how hard he had worked at school and college, he could not decipher the mystical subtext that was scratched beneath the surface of his interactions—those sidewards glances and unspoken words he was supposed to interpret in the heat of the moment. He knew he was missing some of the cues, large chunks of important information that got lost in translation. In response, he was starting to retreat. Too many nights were spent wide-eyed and helpless until the morning chorus of birds signaled another day of exhaustion. He was closing in on himself as if his vision was slowly dimming, the fading light of hope dwindling so subtly that it might be extinguished with the next wind of change. And there had been abundant winds of late. Since the pandemic he could no longer find the outposts of stability—those occasional moments of calm where he could rest from challenges without and within. When he looked back on what he had once known, it was unrecognizable through the squall. He was tired of fighting within himself as much as he was fighting with other people, tired of looking for solutions that seemed endlessly out of reach. From within his confines he could not discern whether this was something of his own creation or circumstances that had been imposed on him.

What could explain the stagnation Sebastian found himself in, fueling endless nights of cursing himself for missed opportunities? Whatever it was, it seemed too deeply entrenched to be a quirk, a matter of unique circumstances coinciding, as illusive an explanation as *fate*. This wasn't a one-off moment of misfortune that might soon blow over, this was a common thread running through his entire life, whether it was his intimate relationships, his friendships, the relationships he had with his family, his work life, or his self-image. All domains were distorted by the same something that was trapping him from within. And this is not just about Sebastian; this thread runs through the lives of all of us.

Within, a prison of our own creation

We are quite inventive beings. For a species that created the Large Hadron Collider, nuclear bomb, light bulb, and augmented reality, we have a considerable depth of imagination. And for all its positive feats, that imagination also has no bounds when it comes to the labyrinthian prisons we create to confine ourselves. We claim to *know* so much about our thoughts that we short-circuit logic, creating further traps out of imprisoning thought patterns. We claim to *know* so much about our emotions that we overreact or underreact, like an unsteady pilot lurching the plane from one extreme to another. And we claim to *know* more than our inner wounded child so that we end up perpetuating the shame and imprisoning messages that were given to us during an adverse childhood. We claim to *know* so much that we create for ourselves an Internal Prison, a steel-bar certainty to guard against our innate aversion to uncertainty. As hunter-gatherers, uncertainty once posed a threat to our survival, and yet now, even though uncertainty might take the more innocuous forms of questions over a career direction or the exit to take on a highway, the same parts of the brain react in the same way: We fear it, and we fill the gap of uncertainty with (sometimes) half-baked knowledge. This knowledge will inevitably be half-baked because we are constantly evolving, and to evolve, we need to rely on the information other people give us, which we do not always have time to verify. And so these Internal Prisons, these mental prisons, are reinforced when we get confirmation from others—confirmation about who we are and how we should be in the world.

Left unchecked, this blind-faith knowledge can lead to disastrous consequences. Like lemmings leaping off a cliff, we follow half-baked concepts simply because other people have done so. Our intolerance of uncertainty can leave us clutching at any form of certainty, and research shows that the certainty of fundamentalist religions, extreme political groups, radical interest groups, and conspiracy theorists can offer a tempting relief to our anxiety. There may be a part of us that knows what is being offered is not the whole truth, because it is so polished and oversimplified, but we prefer claiming to *know* rather than admit that, for a great deal of life, we *cannot know*. Extremism has been around for a long time, but some argue that the surge of digital devices has compounded it. According to the United Nations, the internet is one of the main strategies used to recruit children to extremism. Given our limited options to monitor children's use of online resources, this is particularly troubling. We might have relied on blind-faith knowledge to a lesser degree in the past, but with the evolution of digital devices and other technology, blind-faith knowledge is circulating at an exponential rate, and this takes us away from the wisdom that we can find within.

At one time our knack for invention seemed to be opening the world up to endless opportunities for freedom. The internet helped us to reach corners of the world that we might otherwise never have known about, and so the opportunities to reach beyond our confines seemed infinite. But though our new "toys" might satiate our need for new experiences, stimulating that enjoyable dopamine hit, we ultimately sink back into our own Internal Prison of self-doubt. Within these confines it can be hard to recognize our strengths, and our self-esteem dwindles, taking with it any hope or motivation. Prior to COVID-19 we already were starting to see that our love affair with technology was tantamount to abuse, its draw sucking us in so that we became isolated from ourselves and other people. Our digital devices were becoming our constant companion that seemed to demand more and more of our time, more of our personal information, and seemingly turned us on each other like a sociopath who takes pleasure in causing pain and conflict. And then the pandemic hit and we became more dependent on technology. We found ourselves trapped within another prison, confined to our homes to work, educate our children, and somehow survive. The fault lines of our Internal Prison were further stressed, and we were taken further away from our internal wisdom and natural rhythms.

Sebastian's assumptions about how others perceived him, mostly negative, made him retreat into the confines of a lonely life. Scrolling through social media late into the night, he realized that he hardly ever gave himself the opportunity to meet people who might offer evidence to the contrary, who might show him that others were interesting or interested in him. In his own mind's eye, he had become inadequate, caught in the dim light of limited self-awareness that can discolor even the most vibrant aspects of hope, and he was caught in a cycle of assumptions that kept him cynical and untrusting. Whenever he was forced to interact through necessity (a plumber had to visit, or he was asked a question at the supermarket, for example), his nerves were frayed by the intensity of his emotions. He would be forced to face the uncertainty that he feared, and as sweat trickled down his back, he would feel even more inadequate, even more fearful of life beyond his confines.

We might have reached freedom from the confines of *physical* constraints of the pandemic health restrictions, but we cannot realize the full extent of this freedom when we still confine ourselves within an Internal Prison. As Sebastian attempted to navigate the post-pandemic world, he still struggled to keep hopeful. The schools might have reopened, and the children were finally vaccinated, but unease lingered like a storm cloud. His mind was whirling with phantoms from his own childhood, and even though the initial panic of the pandemic had long since passed, still that sense of danger burned through his nervous system.

Beyond Your Confines will help you to understand that the Internal Prison is your own creation, but so too are the keys that can free your mind. Research shows that rates of anxiety, depression, and relationship conflict decrease when you feel a sense of autonomy and authenticity, when you see the keys to freedom sitting in your hands. The first key to reach beyond the confines of your Internal Prison is to become aware of your mental process. The less aware and in control we are of our internal (mental) state, the more we become a prisoner of it. This blindness leads to greater rates of anxiety, depression, relationship conflict, and other challenges to our mental health. The trouble is, our mental process spins at such a speed that we barely have the chance to register what is going on. It is hard to notice the assumptions we make to plug the gap of uncertainty we fear so greatly, and we do not stop to challenge imprisoning messages from our past that might be patently untrue. *Beyond Your Confines* offers you the opportunity to stop and reflect on the wisdom and natural rhythms that you already have within. *Beyond Your Confines* will help you to understand how you can become trapped in imprisoning thought patterns, emotion dysregulation, intolerance of uncertainty, and low self-esteem. Given the prevalence of mental health challenges since the pandemic, learning how to free your mind from this Internal Prison should be a high priority.

Part of this process of awareness is acknowledging the toxicity and prevalence of trauma. Too many of us dismiss trauma as the one-off catastrophic plane crash, war, or road accident, and yet trauma encompasses so much more. Most mental health professionals would agree that trauma involves a negative event or events that result in a sense of threat or distress. This can include, for example, an accumulation of adverse childhood experiences, something that often causes damage in adulthood, especially if those childhood experiences were inflicted by a caregiver whom you relied upon for survival, and from whom there was no escape. Therefore, to reflect on your internal process, you must be aware of any shame or imprisoning messages from your past, and the needs of your wounded inner child. In recent times, one of the most powerful concepts to help us reach beyond the confines of our Internal Prison is Polyvagal Theory, something we will come back to throughout this book.

The pandemic and post-pandemic world created significant challenges for parents of school-aged children, so there is a whole chapter dedicated to parenting within confines. Parenting poses a unique challenge when those parents have experienced trauma during their own childhood. This can create a wounded inner child that, years later, still needs to be parented, even though that person is now faced with the task of parenting their actual children.

Another key to free your mind is learning the balance between reaching beyond the confines of your Internal Prison and resting within your natural tendency towards introversion or extroversion. This can be particularly hard in societies such as the United States, where there is a bias towards extroversion. To reach beyond your confines requires awareness and acceptance of your own process that is unpolluted or uncoerced by others, which requires curiosity that sits in sharp contrast to judgment. According to Jon Kabat-Zinn in *Mindfulness for Beginners*, mindfulness can offer us "liberation" from the unnecessary suffering of judgment. "We have a powerful innate capacity to hold whatever it is—even terror, despair, and rage—in awareness, and carry it differently," provided we can slow down and redirect our focus away from all the distractions that the world has to offer. As Kabat-Zinn explains, we need to become "open to an interior stillness with no other agenda than to be present for the unfolding of your moments." In an age of polarized views and condemnation that are circulated at the speed of light by our newfound technological *toys*, this slow and steady step towards liberation is much needed.

Without, a prison of structural inequality and privilege

The pandemic and the growth in technology have compounded the evolution of more polarized views. We have seen an uptick in the encroachment of each other's boundaries, discrimination, and outright violence. But we don't just get to blame the new kids on the block. We already had these issues to begin with, and clearly the pandemic hit certain communities harder than others, communities that were already suffering long before the pandemic. It is all very well reaching beyond the confines of an Internal Prison, but we also need to address the External Prison of structural inequality and societal privilege. In *The Gift of Therapy*, Irvin D. Yalom explains that the aim of psychotherapy is to "remove obstacles blocking my patient's path," which means that we need to help people reach beyond their prison of self-construction, yes, but we also need to liberate people from any prison constructed by others. Structural inequality is directly associated with poor mental and physical health in countries such as the United States, and so long as structural inequality remains, the work of a psychotherapist is incomplete. Part of this process of liberation includes acknowledging our own privilege. For example, I must acknowledge my privilege as someone who is white, someone who was given the male label at birth, someone who is college educated, and someone who is a mental health professional. I am part of this structural inequality, and awareness, to monitor how my privilege can harm others, is an ongoing process of discovery.

Too often people turn to mental health practitioners assuming that they hold the answer, or the truth, about their condition. I prefer the perspective of clinical psychologist Catherine Gildiner, who in *Good Morning, Monster* describes psychotherapy as a process where people are "endeavoring to reach some kind of psychological truth" that they can agree on. In this endeavor, psychotherapy and mental health often come down to a balancing act, or an attempt to achieve some sort of equilibrium. In psychotherapy we strive for the Goldilocks of emotions, trying to feel *not too much* but also *not too little,* a balance between down-regulation and up-regulation, a balance between stability and change. To reach beyond your confines means to strike a balance between confinement and freedom, it means challenging yourself to reach beyond what you already know and who you already think you are. So, too, should we strive for a balance between the individual and the society or system within which that individual is located. We cannot understand one without understanding the other, and the health of one is inextricably linked to the health of the other. As Kabat-Zinn postulated in *Meditation is Not What You Think*, "have you noticed how easily we can get caught up in thinking of ourselves as players on an inert stage, as if the world were only 'out there' and not also 'in here'? when, in reality, there is really no separation at all." When it comes to the individual and the environment within which the individual lives, there is a sense of reciprocity, and so we should be asking not only how the world has treated us, but also how we are treating the world. Pointing to just one example of many, global warming, Kabat-Zinn offers a stark warning when he says that "we can no longer afford to ignore this fundamental characteristic of our reciprocity and interconnectedness."

In "Kincentric Ecology: Indigenous Perceptions of the Human Nature Relationship," anthropologist Enrique Salmón highlighted this interconnectedness when he explained the concept of *kincentricity*, the idea that we are all "part of an extended ecological family that shares ancestry and origins. It is an awareness that life in any environment is viable only when humans view the life surrounding them as kin. The kin, or relatives, include all the natural elements of an ecosystem." What we learn from this is that our very own lives consist of a perpetual balancing act between autonomy and interdependency. We, as individuals, are inextricably linked to the system or society within which we exist, and so we cannot strive for the health (mental or physical) of one without the health of the other. We have slowly started to see a shift in this perspective in the mental health profession, from the *individual pathology* perspective to a view of mental health as *inextricably linked to the system or society within which that individual exists*. But still there is work to be done.

How you use *Beyond Your Confines* is not just about you any more than it is just for you. It is also about, and for, society as a whole. Reaching beyond your confines to escape an Internal Prison of your own creation is not just an exercise in individual growth, it also inevitably influences, and is influenced by the External Prison of structural inequality and privilege. For example, to what extent does our intolerance of uncertainty, our need to be right, our lack of imagination, and our encroachment of boundaries, reinforce the walls of that External Prison? To what extent does our depression or low self-esteem play a part in all of this? And the same can be asked about others. To what extent does the intolerance of others, their need to be right, their lack of imagination, their encroachment of our boundaries, or their low self-esteem, keep us imprisoned?

In an age when self-appointed moral arbiters are banning books again, and when the truth about critical race theory seems a little too inconvenient for certain US states, a book is an essential tool to chisel out from our confines and free our minds. We can use this book to learn how we create an Internal Prison out of short-circuited thought patterns, emotion dysregulation, and imprisoning messages from our past. And we can learn that we are also imprisoned by the External Prison of structural inequality and privilege, the walls of which are reinforced by our own intolerances and insecurities. Finally, we can use this book to learn that we are all interconnected, so we all have a part to play in the resultant suffering, and we all play a part in freeing each other from this pain. One big step we can take is to free our minds.

So, the first question you should ask yourself is:

> How are you trapped within your confines, an Internal Prison of your own creation?
> And how can you reach beyond this?

CHAPTER 1

Trapped within your confines

Become the sky. Take an axe to the prison wall. Escape.
- Rumi

“So, what about *you*?” Her eyes pierced me with an intensity that I found unsettling, not least because she was getting to the heart of things. She was getting to the heart of me.
“How do you find yourself trapped? You have spoken about all the mental gymnastics that other people perform to tie themselves in knots, and you are quite adept at recognizing the imprisoning thought patterns or emotion dysregulation of your family and friends, but we have stared out of the window for long enough now. Let’s get to the heart of why you are here. How do you feel trapped, and to what extent is that a prison of your own creation, or confinement imposed by others?”

Nadia was not the first therapist I had ever met with, but she was the first to really challenge me to quit playing games with her. I am not claiming that her approach to therapy was good or bad, but it certainly forced my hand to drop what was, until that point, one of my favorite coping strategies: the art of distraction. And at eighteen years old I was already quite the artist. Even though my father had just died, and I was trying to manage homophobic abuse from others, I could offer quite a colorful array of distractions to postpone the pain that I would inevitably have to face. If it had not been for Nadia’s to-the-point intervention, I might have forever remained trapped within a prison of silence and shame about the grief and abuse I was too afraid and ashamed to speak of.

We are prisoners of our own creation. We fear the reactions of others, we are tarnished by shame, we assume others do not feel the same way we do, and we project on even our most beloved the judgment that we feel towards ourselves. Friedrich Nietzsche put it best when he wrote in *Thus Spoke Zarathustra* that "the worst enemy you can meet will always be yourself," and this is an enemy who stands guard like a night watchman to ensure that you live out the lifetime of limitations to which you have sentenced yourself. Nietzsche wrote *Thus Spoke Zarathustra* in the 1800s, but there was nothing special about that time, no unique turning point to suddenly set us in a new mold as jailor of our own Internal Prison. We have always carried a stick to beat ourselves, as surely as the wheel of the human psyche turns to its own rhythm of fears and assumptions. So, what's new? Enter stage right the villain of *The COVID-19 Pandemic*. Here we are two years later, with restrictions lifted, and we have technically been released from our confines, and yet we stumble and blink into the daylight without a clue how to be. We are still under a lock and key of our own creation. We still lack confidence, we are fighting with each other, and we are overwhelmed by our anxiety. There is no normal to return to; this is a new world which requires a new way of being. We may have already had structural inequality and privilege, worldwide environmental catastrophes, and rapidly evolving digital devices and technology, but combining all this with the pandemic adds stress to the fault lines of our Internal Prisons, causing many to be crushed from within. Two years after the pandemic began, half of adults surveyed by the Kaiser Family Foundation said the pandemic "has had a negative effect on their personal mental health (49%),"— and that is just a small part of it. All this dysregulation and disconnect from our natural harmony—whether from within or the natural world we try to dominate—has widened the gap between rich and poor, distorting privileges beyond measure and cementing us further inside our prisons of polarized thinking and emotion dysregulation. And so the vicious cycle will continue until we stop and regain awareness of how we create an Internal Prison that traps us within our own confines.

In *Meditation is Not What You Think,* Jon Kabat-Zinn claims that we have innate resources that we can use to heal, and that opens us up to the freedom of "relationships with each other and the world." But we can only use these innate resources to their full potential when we free our minds from the darkness of our Internal Prisons. When our natural rhythms are obfuscated by short-circuited thought patterns and an inability to identify or respond to the messages of even our most basic of emotions, we have little hope of a day when we can stumble free of the mixed messages, distorted self-esteem, or electric shock of anxiety that riddle our everyday lives. And the less awareness we have of our Internal Prison, the more confined we are in it and the greater danger that it will crush us from within.

As we are inventive beings, our capacity for creating ways to set our natural rhythms off-kilter seems limitless. We can hyperfocus on something to the point of obsession, or neglect our need for sleep, sustenance, or time and space away from eye-spinning digital devices. We can cling to others like life buoys, threatening to drown them and us with our longing to belong, or we can plow past others without a second thought, hurting them and us in the process. We invent thoughts and beliefs about ourselves and others, and we fear, exaggerate, distort, and compound the natural rhythms of our mind and body. But we are not sitting in a woodworker's studio carving our next inner Pinocchio; we rarely make a conscious decision as to how we should create the next mental gymnastics that can lurch us from panic to ice-cold indifference at the slam of a door. Many of the walls of our Internal Prison are constructed beyond the scope of perception, and it is, in the words of neuroscientist Stephen W. Porges, a case of *neuroception.* Our autonomic nervous system senses whether or not something is a threat, and we respond in a certain way—sometimes in a way that does not liberate us or offer the chance for us to grow but traps us within our confines.

Our autonomic nervous system and *neuroception* - A prison guard in a watchtower

One of the clearest ways to understand how we trap ourselves within an Internal Prison is through Polyvagal Theory. Conceptualized by Stephen W. Porges, Polyvagal Theory claims that before we can even attach meaning to an experience, our autonomic nervous system attempts to keep us safe at all times. And a prison is all about safety, although usually it is designed for the safety of the people outside the prison rather than the person who is trapped within. Like a prison guard in his watchtower, our autonomic nervous system is on a constant surveillance exercise, listening to and watching everything that happens within us, around us, and in relation to others. This prison guard of *neural evaluation of risk* hides beneath our conscious awareness or immediate perception, and so Porges refers to the process as *neuroception* to distinguish it from perception. Even before we can attach meaning to an experience, our autonomic nervous system responds with an adaptive survival response. Neuroception is a prison guard in a watchtower of our autonomic nervous system, and he scans our body and environment for evidence of danger or safety. That *prison guard of neuroception* can spot cues of danger or safety by analyzing voices, facial expression, and other bodily movement, and he does not need to wake the sleeping thought process to evaluate danger or safety. When he hears the right intonation or pitch in someone's voice, for example, he can sense whether that person is safe or unsafe. It explains why a baby coos at a caregiver but cries in the presence of a stranger, and it explains why we immediately run (without thinking) when see a saber tooth tiger. There is no conscious perception, no weighing up of options or experiences we might have had in similar circumstances in the past, we just run.

When I think of the covert nature of surveillance that characterizes neuroception, the way it exists beneath our immediate perception or control, I am struck by the parallels with my own childhood growing up around covert operations that were carried out beyond my perception. I could sense that there was a subplot to my early years as there were gaps in my understanding, threadbare explanations, and half-told stories. For example, to name just two big questions: Why, when we were British, was I born in Helsinki, Finland, and why did we then spend some time—straddling my elementary and high school years—living in Hong Kong? It turns out that my father, and some of my grandparents, had been carrying out covert surveillance exercises to ensure the safety of the United Kingdom, as they had worked for GCHQ, a governmental intelligence and security organization. It turns out that in 1977 they were living in Finland to eavesdrop on what was then the Soviet Union, and in the late eighties, Hong Kong was a British colony, so they were there to spy on China. I remember watching my father's prison-guard focus intensify as they showed footage of the tanks rolling into Tiananmen Square and the words 'Civil War?' flashed on our television screen (I was just annoyed they had interrupted an episode of *Sesame Street*). What I was conscious of and able to control was not the whole picture, any more than the conscious thoughts at any given moment are the whole reality for you. But the fact that I did not *know* the true extent of the covert surveillance makes it no less essential for my safety or survival, and so our lack of conscious awareness of our autonomic nervous system makes it no less essential. Yet we too easily dismiss concepts that are immediately outside of our awareness, dismissing newer concepts like neuroception so they remain within the shadows of cynicism and mistrust. Instead, we prefer to focus on what is immediately within our control, like a baby grabs for the nearest object in part because of their undeveloped eyesight, but also because ignorance of any dangers out of their range of sight is bliss. We would rather feel like we consciously *know* things, even if this knowledge is half-baked or borrowed from others who know as little as we do. Although our *understanding* of neuroception might be as novel as non-fungible art (NFT) or cryptocurrency, the *existence* of it is as old as our nervous system.

In fact, we can go right back to the start of evolution to understand the responses of our mind and body, starting with the most primitive part of our nervous system (estimated to be 500 million years old): the *dorsal vagal pathway*. This part of our nervous system is right at the bottom of our evolutionary ladder, where we respond to extreme danger by *shutting down or immobilization*. We are frozen, numb, or *not there*. We play dead. Think of the times when you have felt overwhelmed or helpless, or when there was a sudden, terrifying event. In those moments, you just might have been in a dorsal vagal state.

Further up the evolutionary ladder, but still pretty ancient, estimated to be 400 million years old, is the *sympathetic nervous system*, which responds to danger by releasing adrenaline. This is our *mobilization response*. Your pupils dilate so you can see more clearly, and your heart starts to pump faster so the blood goes to your limbs, readying you to fight or flee. Think of the times when you have felt flush-faced and sweaty, or nervous, or agitated. No doubt the pandemic created plenty of opportunity to switch into this mode. You may have felt panicky when job losses were announced, for example, or house prices soared so that you could not see a way of ever buying your own home. Or your mind might have started to race during the pandemic, when it was unclear whether your children would ever get vaccinated, or when someone stood too close to you in line at the pharmacy and sweat broke out at the back of your neck as you struggled between saying something and remaining quiet. In those moments, your autonomic nervous system was readying you to *fight or flee*.

Finally, at the top of the evolutionary ladder, a significantly more youthful age of 200 million years old, you find the *social engagement system* which, Porges writes, "responds to cues of safety" and supports a feeling of being socially connected. Think of times when you have felt safe and calm or relaxed. Think of times when you have enjoyed doing things that give you pleasure, such as playing music or relaxing with your loved ones. In those moments, you might have been activating your *ventral vagal system.*

The top and bottom of the ladder—the shutdown response and the socially engaged response—are attributable to two pathways within the vagus nerve. The vagus nerve is part of the parasympathetic nervous system; the shutdown pathway is called the dorsal vagal pathway, and the social engagement pathway is called the ventral vagal pathway. According to Porges, the vagus nerve runs down "from the brain stem at the base of the skull"—through the lungs, heart, diaphragm, and stomach—and up, "connecting with nerves in the neck, throat, eyes, and ears." This explains why many therapists who use Polyvagal Theory stress the importance of simple exercises, like breathing, tapping, and vocal toning. These strategies are focused on activating the *social engagement system*, otherwise known as the ventral vagal pathway. Porges claims that we are at our optimum state for "health, growth, and restoration" when the ventral vagus is activated. The vagus nerve is often referred to as a *neural brake*, slowing your body down so that you can connect with others. All of this shows us that an understanding of Polyvagal Theory helps us see how the surveillance system of our autonomic nervous system can imprison us but also help us to reach beyond our confines by connecting with others in an essential process of co-regulation.

If our autonomic nervous system is a prison guard who tries to keep us safe, how can we say that he traps us? Isn't he, instead, a watchful guardian? The answer can be found when our sense of safety and sense of connection are misaligned. If we sense danger when there is none, our autonomic nervous system goes into a protective mode of shutdown or fight-or-flight. This isn't very useful if we are trying to strike up a business relationship in the boardroom and suddenly we are sweating or on the edge of a panic attack. Then we are trapped by our watchful prison guard because it is trying to keep us safe when there isn't any danger. Remember, this is all beyond our immediate perception, so what we sense or neurocept does not always match reality. When there is a misalignment between our environment and what we neurocept as safety or danger, our prison guard autonomic nervous system can become overly zealous and trap us in a state of shutdown or fight-or-flight.

When our autonomic nervous system becomes an overzealous prison guard—Beyond our window of tolerance

COVID-19 was not the first health crisis the world has faced. The 1918 influenza pandemic killed fifty million worldwide, and what was striking about that pandemic was that it hit the young, people between the ages of fifteen and forty-five, the hardest. When it comes to health crises, young people in this age group are not the obvious victims; it is usually the very old or the very young. So, what could explain this anomaly? In *Pox Americana: The Great Smallpox Epidemic of 1775-82,* Elizabeth Fenn explains that "the patients' own robust immune systems were part of the problem, unleashing a torrent of virus-fighting molecules called cytokines that latched on to lung tissue causing lethal damage." Their own internal process was literally killing them from within. They were trying to handle the threat to their health by using their own built-in immune system, and yet it was so strong in these young people that it was killing them.

In a similar way, our own internal mental process often develops to protect us, to keep us safe from harm, and to attempt to meet our needs. In response to a perceived threat, we can *shut down*, or we can mobilize our heart rate, so we are ready to *fight or flee*. In addition to fight, flight, or freeze, we can also *fawn*, which means, in the words of psychotherapist Peter Walker (in "Codependency, Trauma and the Fawn Response"), we adapt to "servitude, ingratiation, and forfeiture of any needs that might inconvenience and ire" the aggressor. These are all protective responses when we sense danger, and because they take a great deal of energy, they are not supposed to be used continuously. However, we can end up stuck, continuously responding with *fight, flight, freeze, or fawn* when we are triggered (when something happens that reminds us of a past event that might have been overwhelming or traumatic, for example). When we get stuck in this protective response, we can end up exhausted, depleted, depressed, anxious, or burned out.

Without learning about how (and why) our mind and body responds to certain circumstances, we become our own internal jailor. Without awareness of our internal processes, or by adding contaminants such as adverse childhood experiences, what were once protective internal processes can go into overdrive, increasing the danger that they will end up harming (or even killing) the host. It is clear to see the parallels between this and the 1918 influenza pandemic, when the immune systems of young people (the protective internal processes) went into overdrive and ended up killing millions.

When we activate our *social engagement system*, it is possible to connect with others, but it is not always inevitable. *Ideally*, we use things like tone of voice, facial expression, and body language to send *cues of safety and invitations* for connection, communicating, "one nervous system to another, that it is safe to approach and come into relationship," Porges writes. *Ideally*, our response matches the environment, where we fight, flee, or shutdown in the face of danger, and connect with ourselves and others when it is safe. But sometimes there is a *misalignment* between the reality of our environment, and then the safety responses are activated and we cannot stop fighting, fleeing, fawning, or shutting down when there is no danger to be found. Then we remain trapped within our own Internal Prison.

There is often this sort of misalignment when we have experienced trauma. As we saw earlier in this book, trauma includes any negative event or events that result in a sense of threat or distress, and this can include an accumulation of adverse childhood experiences. When we have experienced trauma, no matter how many years ago, it can be easy to slip into a state of dysregulation. We feel trapped on a bewildering seesaw of reliving the events in one moment—with all the nerve-frying fear that burns us—to being ice-cold with the detached numbness in the next moment, which appears to others emotionless or uncaring. In *Trauma and Recovery*, psychiatrist Judith Herman refers to this as "the dialectic of trauma," or in the words of George Orwell, "doublethink" (*Trauma and Recovery*, Judith Herman).

Another way to describe the dialectic of trauma is as a prison of hyperarousal and hypoarousal. When you are *hyperaroused* you are stuck in the sympathetic nervous system state of *mobilization*. You feel upset by things that wouldn't usually upset you, you are restless, your limbs are twitchy, you feel angry, you feel on edge, and you judge yourself harshly for what may, to others, seem like minor mistakes. Some view hyperarousal as a means of coping with what seems overwhelming; all that excess energy we invest in worrying makes us feel like we are doing something about the dangers, and it can distract us from other, more overwhelming feelings.

Equally dysregulated, but in the polar-opposite way, when you are hypoaroused you feel detached, depressed, numb, and unmotivated. You are stuck in the dorsal vagal state of *immobilization*. There is a difference between the inner stillness that Jon Kabat-Zinn refers to in *Mindfulness for Beginners*, and the complete shutdown of our dorsal vagal response, with one being minutely aware of that stillness and calm that allow for healing, and the other a deathly numbness that blocks off any awareness. One opens us up to the hope of connection with others, the other shuts us off from any hope of mutual co-regulation; one gives us freedom from within, the other confines us further within a trap of stagnation. *Dissociation* is another way to refer to feeling detached, depressed, numb, and unmotivated. Dissociation is a coping strategy that might have once helped us survive a trauma but now leaves us feeling stuck in a blank-minded, detached, or apparently feelingless state. All too often people misunderstand survivors of trauma. They see the blank face of dissociation or hypoarousal, or they see the angry face of hyperarousal, and they do not appreciate that someone might be reliving a past trauma.

To free ourselves of the Internal Prisons of hyperarousal or hyperarousal, we need to develop an ability to keep within an optimum level of activation, which therapists refer to as the *window of tolerance*. You are aware, alert, engaged in the present, but not so much that you are hyperaroused and not so little that you are hypoaroused. Too often we are either unaware of our emotions, or we judge ourselves for our fears and distress. Either can push us further out of the window of tolerance and into either hyperarousal or hypoarousal. With the help of a therapist, you can expand your window of tolerance, becoming more aware, and more accepting, of the emotions that come up. As you expand your window of tolerance, you are increasingly able to tolerate emotions that were once overwhelming. You can expand your window of tolerance by slowing down to mindfully notice what is going on for you and naming those feelings, sometimes even out loud. You can start to train your brain not to fear, avoid, or shut down in the face of these emotions, but to experience them, slowly and gently, and survive.

In *Waking the Tiger*, psychologist Peter Levine refers to the concept of *pendulation*. Levine explains that your nervous system has a natural ebb and flow to it, a balance between *expansion* and *contraction*. However, when you have experienced trauma, your body can become *locked up* or *stuck*.

A therapist can help you to slowly attune to your body, so you learn the sensations associated with feeling *okay* or *calm*. This is known as *resourcing*. When you learn a sense of presence or grounding in your body, your nervous system can tolerate a little stress without getting stuck because you can come back to a sense of calm or *okayness* in your body. You can learn to pendulate between these feelings of *contraction* and *expansion* without getting stuck. In other words, you can stay within your window of tolerance without becoming hyperaroused or hypoaroused. Levine's concept of this natural rhythm of expansion and contraction is just another one of those balancing acts that we encounter in this book, a balancing act that offers just one of the many keys to release you from the confines of your Internal Prison.

A prison of nerves—the unsteady pilot

We will forever remain trapped within our Internal Prison if we don't learn as many forms of emotion regulation as possible. We have seen a few examples already, and we will continue to review more throughout *Beyond Your Confines*. Without an ability to regulate our emotions, we become like a pilot who is unaware of the purpose of all the controls in their cockpit, who is too distracted or disconnected to notice the warning signs, or who grips the controls too tightly, overreacting or underreacting and lurching the plane from one extreme to another.

Consider Cassie. When she walked into the playground, her heart started to race. She felt as if all eyes were on her, scrutinizing her every move and waiting for her to trip and fall. She could feel her throat tighten as her heart pounded harder. Her breathing became shallow, and she felt sweat trickling down her back. Fears were gathering like a storm in her mind, making her believe that she would end up passed out on the ground in front of everyone. She was certain that her children would end up humiliated and without any friends, all because she could not walk onto a playground with calm and ease.

The trouble with Cassie was that she reacted to her increased heart rate with fear and trepidation, assuming the worst would happen and trying to fight her feelings. An increased heart rate can be helpful to motivate us or focus our attention on a challenge, but Cassie was fighting it with her mind and body, only increasing the chances of a panic attack or ongoing anxiety. Over subsequent weeks, Cassie started making excuses about work meetings when it came to school dismissal, forcing her partner to take on that particular parenting role. While this might have given Cassie temporary relief, she was depriving herself of a learning opportunity. Sometimes what is needed to regulate our emotions is to gently lean into the discomfort, like surfing a wave, noticing the peak of the sensations, but staying with it so we can also experience the subsiding of the feelings. Our brain has learned a new experience in which we have mastered our mind and body. Our brain learns that the catastrophe did not occur, and we were able to handle this anxiety-provoking experience.

When we remain trapped within our confines, we deprive ourselves of this opportunity to learn and grow. Since the pandemic, many of us are still choosing to distract ourselves or avoid the discomfort, trapped by a fear that we might be overwhelmed if we lean into the discomfort. There are limitless ways to distract and avoid, whether through more obvious forms such as alcohol, drugs, or food, or less obvious forms such as excessive work or exercise or overinvolvement in the drama of other people's lives. When you distract yourself or avoid a situation that usually provokes distress, you engage in what is called *safety behavior*. You believe that you are keeping safe when in reality you are making yourself more vulnerable to your emotions. Cassie's safety behavior was avoidance of the other parents in the school playground, and Marcus's safety behavior was not volunteering to deliver a presentation at work. Paul's safety behavior was lying and claiming that he was too busy to meet up with his family, and Suzanne's safety behavior was speaking quietly when she attended her college reunion. The most overlooked form of safety behavior, and a silent plea for help rather than admiration, is being socially performative and overbearing. When he was at work meetings, Tommy would infuriate his coworkers with endless accounts of his latest holidays, or house renovations, or the latest accolades bestowed upon his three children.

For survivors of trauma, avoidance of emotions can become a habitual coping strategy because, as Bessel A. van der Kolk described in *The Body Keeps the Score*, trauma survivors "feel unsafe inside their bodies: The past is alive in the form of gnawing interior discomfort. Their bodies are constantly bombarded by visceral warning signs, and, in an attempt to control these processes, they often become expert at ignoring their gut feelings and in numbing awareness of what is played out inside. They learn to hide from their selves." When trauma is a result of adverse childhood experiences, emotion dysregulation can be particularly acute. Adverse childhood experiences include humiliation at the hands of your caregivers, your caregivers swearing at you or making you afraid you might be hurt, your caregivers' failure to meet your physical needs, or growing up in a family where you do not feel special. Adverse childhood experiences also include sexual abuse (from an adult or from another child who was at least five years older than you), your caregivers separating or divorcing, witnessing domestic violence, and someone in your household struggling with mental health issues, drink, drugs, or going to prison. The Center on the Developing Child, part of Harvard University, explains that an adverse childhood deprives our brain of necessary positive stimulation, and results in an activation of the body's stress response, "flooding the developing brain with potentially harmful stress hormones." The resulting toxic stress "can undermine the development of the body's stress response systems, and affect the architecture of the developing brain, the cardiovascular system, the immune system, and metabolic regulatory controls."

There once was a time when avoidance, in the form of confinement, was a common approach to ill health. In *Recovery: The Lost Art of Convalescence*, Dr Gavin Francis, a doctor in Scotland, explains that doctors would once confine their patients to bed for weeks. Today, the consensus is that this generally causes more harm than good. In much the same way with our mental health, *wholesale* confinement, in the form of avoidance or distraction—whether in the form of a bottle of whiskey, complete absorption in video games, or selling your home and retreating to a Buddhist monastery for the rest of your life—is not beneficial for most people. To reach beyond the confines of our dysregulated emotions, one approach is to expose ourselves—gently and slowly, and ideally with the help of a trained healthcare professional—to some of the things that cause our anxiety. A therapist can help you to gradually give up the *safety behavior* that was never really keeping you safe. Instead of avoidance, we need to strike a balance between feeling too much and not feeling enough, or we need to *pendulate*, in the words of Peter Levine. This is an ongoing process, and the greater awareness and acceptance we have of our emotional state, the more we will become the steady pilot who can surf the waves of life's turbulence.

Regulating and co-regulating our way in and out of confinement

In 1980 the World Health Organization announced that "the world and all its peoples have won freedom from smallpox." After killing 300 million people in the twentieth century, smallpox was no more, the first time such a global threat to human health had been eradicated. This achievement was made possible because of the *collaboration and cooperation* between countries around the world. What this tells us is a story of hope through the power of connection and collaboration with others. When it comes to reaching beyond the confines of our Internal Prison of emotion dysregulation, many neuroscientists, psychologists, and psychiatrists offer an equally hopeful message of connection.

According to Charles Cooley, we have a greater understanding of ourselves through the eyes of others, and this self-identity grows as we interact with more people, a concept known as the looking-glass self. According to Kabat-Zinn, the give-and-take of "relationality" gives us "a place in this world, how we know in our hearts that we actually do belong and make a difference." Too often our concept of mental health, and our understanding of the mind, adopts a focus on the individual, and yet Dan Siegel, clinical professor of psychiatry at UCLA School of Medicine, defines the mind as "an embodied and relational process that regulates the flow of energy and information." The mind cannot be viewed in isolation as just brain activity, or things that happen within the skull. "Human connections shape neural connections, and each contributes to mind," Siegel writes in *The Developing Mind*. Our minds, and our mental health, exist in relation to others.

According to Porges, "we come into the world wired to connect," and we connect with others through a process of "reciprocal regulation of our autonomic states." We have the ability to regulate our emotions, but we also have the ability to *co-regulate*. As polyvagal expert Deb Dana explains in *The Polyvagal Theory in Therapy*: "co-regulation creates a physiological platform of safety that supports a psychological story of security that then leads to social engagement." This process of co-regulation can occur between parent and child, as the parent rocks a baby, soothes a child's fears, or sings or speaks to them with just the right intonation or pitch. But co-regulation is not confined to childhood; it is an ongoing process of soothing and calming we engage in as we interact with each other, talking or sighing or nodding encouragingly to each other. Two friends can co-regulate as much as two lovers, as can a therapist and their client, and even a pet and their owner. When we are supported by co-regulating relationships, we can develop resilience that enables us to reach beyond the confines of any Internal Prison we may have constructed, and we can seek out connection. In sharp contrast, a dysregulated relationship of violence or intimidation can lock our nervous system in a protective stance. Our sympathetic nervous system increases the adrenalin as we switch into fight-or-flight mode, or in the face of ultimate danger, we adopt a shutdown state of numbness or disconnection. Our lives are a perpetual balancing act of connection and protection, switching in and out of our confines depending upon how we *neurocept* apparent safety or danger.

When the *social engagement system* is activated—in other words when we are in a ventral vagal state—co-regulation is possible, where we connect with others "to soothe and be soothed, to talk and listen, to offer and receive, to fluidly move in and out of connection," Dana explains. In contrast, when we are isolated from other people, we can suffer. We only need to remember how we felt during the lockdown of 2020 to know how lonely life can get. As Dana points out, "being separated from social connection, isolated from other people, is a life-long risk factor affecting both physical and emotional health," and studies show that "social disconnection and social exclusion activate the same pain pathways as experiences of injury," and a "lonely autonomic nervous system moves into habitual patterns of adaptive defense, making the physiological state of safety unavailable." When we are in the ventral vagal state, we can nourish and be nourished by the reciprocity that defines the relationship of connectedness. When our autonomic nervous systems communicate with each other, through a back-and-forth sense of attunement and resonance, we can feel nourished.

Think of the times you have just hung out with your partner, your children, or your closest friends. Did you feel a sense of the "calm, happy, meditative, engaged, attentive, active, interested, excited, passionate, alert, ready, relaxed, savoring, and joyful" states that Porges uses to define the characteristics of the *social engagement system*? In this ventral vagal state we soften our tone, we have a slower heart rate, and we can even see it in each other's eyes. The ventral vagus is the compassion nerve, but it is not about trying to be the next great saint. When we are in this state, we can direct the compassion inwards, freeing ourselves from our own Internal Prisons.

What Polyvagal Theory teaches us is that our autonomic nervous system and *neuroception* is beyond our perception, but this does not mean we are beyond the hope of change. Our autonomic nervous system can imprison us, but we can use Polyvagal Theory as a key to free our minds. As Porges points out, the "autonomic nervous system can be reshaped toward safety and connection." Within the safety of a therapeutic relationship, we can learn to move fluidly up and down the ladder of our autonomic nervous system as the context requires, from connection, into a protective stance, and back to connection again.

Imprisoning messages from your past

If co-regulation creates a physiological platform of safety, imprisoning messages from our past can destroy that security, deterring us from social engagement and leaving us trapped from within. We all grow up with messages from our past. Ideally, we grow up with messages, communicated explicitly and implicitly by our caregivers, that we have value, that we are loved, that we are lovable, and that we are safe. The reality is sometimes far from this, and we grow up with imprisoning messages that create unhelpful beliefs about ourselves, about others, and about the world around us. For example, *I am unsafe, other people are unsafe, I am defective* or *bad* or *shameful*, and *I am powerless*. From a young age we can develop these unrealistic and negative beliefs to help us survive, to help us turn a blind eye to a more painful reality that paints our caregiver as unable or unwilling to protect us, or love us, or see any worth in us. For example, we might prefer to accept the belief that *I am unlovable and bad*, that *I am somehow at fault*, instead of accepting the more frightening reality that the person who was supposed to keep us safe, who we, as a child, depended upon for survival, was either unable or unwilling to love or protect us.

No matter how many years pass, we can remain trapped within the confines of these mistaken beliefs. Deep in our core we agree with that caregiver that we really are worthless or bad, and so we live according to our label. Left unchecked, this can color any adult relationship we attempt to form, and ultimately a self-fulfilling prophecy is created, where we start to see, in our adult life "evidence" of these mistaken beliefs from our childhood.

Just as we saw with the 1918 pandemic, our own internal defenses, what mental processes we developed to keep us safe, can actually make things worse in the face of a new challenge. Take, for example, the COVID-19 pandemic and the stay-at-home orders. For many, this will have reinforced unhelpful beliefs such as *I am unsafe* and *I am powerless,* and it might also have triggered old responses of hyperarousal or hypoarousal. For example, according to van der Kolk, hyperarousal interferes with your "ability to make calm and rational assessments" and you end up responding "to threats as emergencies requiring action rather than thought." To remain constantly vigilant—even at home, where work and education of school-aged children were temporarily relocated—was exhausting for the nervous system. There was no longer any safe or calm place to rebalance the nervous system, and in this heightened state, I know many who experienced irreversible harm to their mental well-being, careers, and personal relationships.

Just as our immune systems may overreact to a virus, in adulthood we can *overcorrect* the experiences we endured as a child. For example, we never want to feel overwhelmed by another person again and so we can push people away with the use of avoidance or zealously protect our rights with anger and frustration. Shame might silence us about the trauma we experienced and so we end up isolating ourselves under the assumption that there is safety in our confines. This may be true temporarily, but eventually it will only concretize the belief that the whole world is unsafe and all people are untrustworthy, or that the whole of you is unlovable. The Center on the Developing Child, part of Harvard University, refers to early experiences as "the development of brain architecture, which provides the foundation for all future learning, behavior, and health." If we have grown up without a caring or attentive caregiver, "the brain's architecture does not form as expected, which can lead to disparities in learning and behavior." As the Center explains: "serious early adversity or trauma can lead to higher levels of stress, higher risk of stress-related health difficulties and mood disorders, greater difficulty modulating and accurately appraising emotion, and compromised executive function abilities."

If we are to have any hope of challenging the imprisoning messages from our past, we need to reach beyond the confines of our experiences to date and learn to connect with others. That way, we might find evidence to the contrary that *I am powerless*, *others are unsafe*, and *the world is overwhelming*. We need to replace the imprisoning messages of the past with new, more helpful (and realistic), messages. *I am unsafe*, *I am powerless*, and *I am worthless* are too absolute, too black-and-white, to be realistic. And if they are unrealistic, they are far from helpful. You need concepts about yourself, and about the world around you, that enable you to keep your eyes wide open to reality. *I am unsafe* is too absolute to be realistic and helpful because there will be situations where you are safe; and in situations where you are uncertain, you have means of keeping yourself safe. It is unrealistic and unhelpful to carry the belief that *I am powerless* because you have a certain measure of power to varying degrees, depending on the situation. Sometimes releasing yourself from your Internal Prison can involve a simple exercise where you identify all the parts of your life where you do have power and control, life buoys of hope and certainty in this sea of perpetual change that is our post-pandemic world. The final belief, that *I am worthless*, can often be the hardest message to challenge, especially if it has been reinforced by abusive caregivers. When I work on this with a client, it can feel like every aspect of their life has been tarred with the same brush of shame and guilt. An important part of this work involves a distinction made between *who I am* and *what happened to me*.

But how can we connect with others and find evidence to dispute our unrealistic beliefs when these imprisoning messages can become so confining? The answer can be discovered from another health crisis, the smallpox epidemic of the 1700s, when Revolutionary War soldiers realized that if they took virus-loaded material from one smallpox victim and rubbed it into an incision in the flesh of a healthy soldier, most of those soldiers developed an immunity to smallpox. This created a sense of safety that did not rely on any mask or confinement within the home; these soldiers carried that freedom from within. In the same way, imprisoning messages such as *I am unsafe*, *I am powerless*, and *I am worthless* are assumptions that need to be disproven, and just as a little chafing promotes the growth of scar tissue to cover a deeper wound, so too can a little amount of anxiety-provoking experience promote the growth of hope for a different set of messages, a newfound belief that *I am safe*, *I have power*, and *I have value*. Scientists once believed that our brain's potential for change, in the form of the creation of new neurons, was confined to the immediate aftermath of birth. But now neuroscientists understand that the brain can create new neurons, neural pathways, and neural connections throughout our life; this is the concept of *neuroplasticity*. With new experiences, our brain can learn new ways of being, and we can develop a more realistic, and a more hopeful, self-identity.

A healing therapeutic relationship can be a starting point as much as a trusted friend or family member, and from within this new experience, we can learn that we can trust and feel safe, and that others can be trustworthy and safe.

Imprisoning thought patterns

Remember how co-regulation creates a physiological platform of safety, and how imprisoning messages from our past can destroy that security? So too can unhelpful thought patterns, leaving us trapped within our Internal Prison. You can become your own jailor, and no matter how much you try to regulate your emotions, you will remain trapped by the dead-end logic of imprisoning thought patterns. As Shakespeare wrote in *Hamlet*, "there is nothing either good or bad, but thinking makes it so."

Roger couldn't face a return to the office—not after two years of working from home. He had gotten used to spending time with his wife and children, and he had already started plans for a renovation of his home that he assumed he would oversee. When his boss made the announcement, and Roger saw the date looming in his calendar, all he could think of was the unclean and unsafe daily commute on public transport and what little time he would get to rest before he had to return to work the following morning. The worst of it was having to keep a smile on his face when he was around colleagues whom he mostly found boring, and, in one or two cases, infuriating. When the day finally arrived and he put on his suit and walked into the office, his stomach dropped as he saw his colleagues' eyes scanning him. No doubt, he assumed, they were judging him for putting on so much weight in the previous two years. He started to feel even more overwhelmed when he thought about his boss seeing how his coworkers judged him, and he believed that no matter how much extra work he put in, this would inevitably mean that he never got a promotion or bonus. By the time Roger returned home that evening, he was struggling to fight back tears, certain that his wife would not appreciate his inability to handle one day back at the office when she had not stopped seeing patients in person at her dental practice.

By the time he told his brother about all of this, he was in pieces. He could barely eat, he had started drinking again, and his sleeping routine was shot. Roger had made a series of assumptions about his colleagues, his boss, and his wife, and yet there was the distinct possibility that none of them were true, and the intensifying depression that was dragging him down was because of his imprisoning thought patterns. Roger compounded his misery when he started to take these assumed reactions of his coworkers, boss, and wife and use them to judge himself as a *failure*. No matter which part of his life he looked at, this core belief tended to trap him in a pit of depression.

There are numerous imprisoning thought patterns, but many therapists recognize ten that worsen how we feel about a situation, and the most popular expert on this is David D. Burns, who wrote *The Feeling Good Handbook.*

It can be quite humbling to realize that we are all in this together, that imprisoning thought patterns can trap anyone, whether a banker, teacher, social worker, or the Dalai Lama. As a result, we can share these with our children, so they do not feel so alone when they start to fall into these traps.

**

Respite – Ten imprisoning thought patterns

1. *The tyranny of the shoulds* – This is when you become distressed because life does not live up to your unrealistic expectations. For example, you believe that you *should* be faultless, or others *should* be on time, or you *must* have a job by the end of the summer.
Whether it is a *should* or a *must*, the result is the same, and that is a life of rigidity. Karen Horney was the first to

introduce the phrase *the tyranny of the shoulds* in *Neurosis and Human Growth: The Struggle Toward Self-Realization*, and ever since, therapists have encouraged people to adopt a more flexible approach to life in order to reach beyond the confines of this imprisoning thought pattern.

2. *Emotional reasoning* – Just because you *feel* it is so, does not make it true. Emotions are useful to guide you, but they are not our only sources of information. For example, you feel scared, and so you believe you are under threat; or you feel uncertain about someone, so you convince yourself that they cannot be trusted.
To reach beyond the confines of this imprisoning thought pattern, Marsha M. Linehan, a psychologist who created dialectical behavior therapy (DBT), introduced us to the *Wise Mind*, a balance of the *Emotion Mind* and the *Reasonable Mind.* In *DBT Skills Training Manual,* Linehan explained that we can trap ourselves in a heartstrong state if we lean too much into our Emotion Mind, following impulses and desires with carefree abandon, only to quickly regret our fecklessness when we have no job or marriage or home to live in. Likewise, if we lean too heavily into the Reasonable Mind and develop a headstrong state, our decisions will be based on logic without the important element of motivation, love, or desires. We need a balance of the two, and sometimes we need to make a conscious effort to seek out information from one mind if we are used to listening to the other. The balanced state, listening to both the Emotion Mind and the Reasonable Mind, results in the Wise Mind.

3. *Personalization* – When the client decides to end their contract with you, when the parents in your children's grade are not getting along, and when your elderly parents are seeming a little sadder than they used to be, do you

end up pointing the finger at no one but yourself? These are all painful examples of the imprisoning thought pattern of personalization.

It is understandable that we need to step up and take responsibility, but to balance this, if we burden ourselves with everyone's responsibilities, we will forever remain trapped within our confines. Point the finger of responsibility at yourself if you want, but only if you also find equal responsibility in other people involved and other factors. And remember: some things are just bad luck. I always remember a fellow therapist switching the language a little by saying "instead of *I failed in this relationship*, you can say *the relationship failed.*"

4. *All-or-nothing thinking* – This is throwing the baby out with the bathwater or failing to see the subtle shades of gray that are between the polar opposites of black and white. You take an unhelpfully wholesale approach to things, believing that if you make one mistake at work then you are condemned to a life of failure, or that if someone lets you down just once, you have to end the relationship.

To reach beyond the confines of this imprisoning thought pattern, identify the middle ground between all or nothing.

5. *Mind reading and assumptions* — We inevitably make assumptions because we simply have not got time to fill every gap in the information chain. Much of this book is about striking a healthy balance, so we need to continually monitor how far these assumptions are likely to take us from reality.

When it comes to mind reading, we can sometimes project onto someone else what we are thinking or feeling, so the more we are aware of our own processes, the better we can separate those from the thoughts and feelings of other people. *Beyond Your Confines* will bring you one step closer to gaining that self-awareness.

6. *Catastrophic thinking* — Why would you ever leave the house if you thought that your children were going to be snatched from you or run over by a truck? Why go for that promotion when you are certain that you will make a mistake that will result in a federal indictment? Why dare to fall in love when you can see your love interest leaving you heartbroken? Such catastrophes are possible but not certain, and if we all lived like this, we would forever trap ourselves in a prison of distorted thinking. Most of us do not think like this all the time, but we have our moments, particularly when we feel tired and drained, and particularly hot on the heels of a pandemic.
To reach beyond the confines of this imprisoning thought pattern, reality test these potential catastrophes. How likely is it that they will happen? And for the things most likely to happen, what safeguards do you have in place, and what strengths and resources do you have at your disposal to survive them? Let's also not fall into the trap of thinking that each possibility is catastrophic. That person who ends up leaving you might be the last person you need in your life, and like a flower that has been deadheaded, space might have been cleared for a better person to take their place.

7. *Overgeneralization* — Your in-laws are *always* criticizing you, and your mother *never* helps with the kids, and your sister *always* gets the attention when she is awarded a promotion at work.
You overgeneralize every bump in the road as a sign that the whole cliff face is about to collapse into an abyss of failure, and yet to reach beyond the confines of this imprisoning thought pattern, you simply need to drill into

the details. Does one criticism wipe away the years of love your in-laws have shown you in their own, crabby ways?

8. *Cyclops* — Beware the one-eyed monster from Greek mythology, because on your more vulnerable days you might end up acting a little like it. If you focus on one negative aspect of your life, you can end up obsessing over it so much that it keeps you up at night and you become overly sensitive, believing that everyone is judging you for it.

A simple way to reach beyond these confines is to take a survey of other people's perspective of you. What do they notice, and what are the top strengths and weaknesses on their list? Often you will find that the one feature you were focusing on was far less important to them than to you.

9. *Bargain-basementing the positives* — You have been in the same career for over fifteen years, and your initial enthusiasm has long since disappeared. Every day you log onto your computer you resent it, and you end up treating every advantage of this secure position in the company, these years of experience that have given you the skills and experience to become invaluable to the company and a worthy new recruit for a headhunter, as *bargain-basement positives.*

To reach beyond the confines of this imprisoning thought pattern, carry out a cost-benefit analysis, including the short- and long-term costs versus the short- and long-term benefits of making a change. Also, if all your needs are not being met—for example in the excitement department—perhaps these can be met through means beyond your work life.

10. *Blindfolding with labels* — In *Beyond the Blue* I explained how the male label can blindfold us to the

reality that people who are male labeled suffer from anxiety, depression, and trauma. As a result, the male label serves as an obstacle to access to mental health care, especially when it intersects with other labels. For example, due to the racism, transphobia, or homophobia of a healthcare professional, someone might not get the help they need because of unhelpful labels that obscure needs hidden beneath the labels.

In a similar way, people can remain trapped within an Internal Prison when they label themselves as a "loser" or "failure." Using pejorative labels to refer to yourself gets you nowhere, and even seemingly positive labels such as "the sporty one" or "the sociable one" can feel like a prison, trapping us behind the solid bars of expectation to be a certain way instead of allowing the full scope of our personality to run free.

**

For the last twenty years, Miguel has worked in the facilities department of an investment bank. He is dedicated to his career, hard-working, and he always follows the rules. This makes him a valuable asset to the bank, but his rule-adherence causes him intense frustration when he witnesses other workers at the bank willingly flout the rules that he holds dear. For example, some coworkers refuse to adhere to company guidelines about the use of company equipment, or the need for a security pass to gain access to the building. Recently Miguel's frustration has been mounting because he is expected to turn a blind eye to the more senior rule breakers, who are viewed by leadership at the bank as too important to upset. When Miguel would talk about this with his friends, he would pound his fist, shouting, "They *should* follow the rules, pure and simple. Why can't people get that into their thick skulls? Everywhere I turn there are people screwing me over, why can't everyone just do what they are supposed to do?" No doubt you will recognize this imprisoning thought pattern as the *tyranny of the shoulds*," a tendency to hold rigid expectations about life. The trouble is, life likes to surprise us, and Miguel does not like surprises.

What makes things worse for Miguel is his overwhelming sense of inadequacy. His father had often told Miguel that he could be a banker, but he could never afford to pay for school and so he ended up without a bachelor's degree. Instead, Miguel started his own facilities company from scratch. He made a success of his business and by any objective standards was far from a failure, but because he *felt* like that, he was convincing himself that he really was a failure. This is an example of *emotional reasoning*.

Miguel is not alone. We all grow up with certain beliefs, assumptions, and fears, and we can all become trapped by imprisoning thought patterns. While we need to learn that there is life beyond this Internal Prison of our own creation, there will be times when we need to rest within the confines of what we know, finding safety from within.

So how can we recognize when enough is enough, when we can rest for now, and accept what *is* rather than strive for what *could be*?
When does confinement work?

CHAPTER 2

When confinement works

We have seasons when we flourish and seasons when the leaves fall from us,
revealing our bare bones. Given time, they grow again.
- Katherine May

For all the racism that colored the messages of the pandemics of 1918 and 2020—calling the 1918 pandemic the *Spanish flu*, and the messaging in 2020 when some used the inaccurate phrase the *China virus*—one truth remained: Confinement works. Both pandemics were created by travel, with the troops in 1918 spreading influenza, and globalization in 2020 spreading the COVID-19 virus. Therefore, active measures to confine people saved many lives. Stay-at-home orders were issued, businesses and schools closed, and travel ground to a halt. Do you remember reports of the clearer skies over what is usually heavily polluted cities such as Los Angeles, New York, and Beijing? Similarly, we also sometimes need to stop and confine ourselves, to create a space within which we rest, giving ourselves room to breathe. The virtue of this can be seen in the natural world as much as our world of mental construction.

When I work with survivors of trauma, we often need to confine the limits of our work because doing too much too soon can end up overwhelming the client's autonomic nervous system. As we saw earlier, with psychologist Peter Levine's concept of *pendulation*, you need to *slowly* attune to your body, so you learn to pendulate between feelings of *contraction* and *expansion* without getting stuck. And so *confinement* can take the form of *resourcing*, when you attune to your body and learn the sensations associated with feeling *okay* or *calm*. When we do this, sometimes I help my clients to visualize a safe or calm place, or even a container to hold the distressing material, at least for a moment. We can become quite inventive when it comes to creating this container, which can take the form of a solid safe, high-security prison, or even a huge warehouse which is carried by a helicopter and dropped out in the middle of the ocean.

Confinement also works when we refer to a cycle that can be broken. It is a hopeful message that we can stop the cycle of adverse childhood experiences, for example, by parenting our own children in sharp contrast to the abusive parenting we might have experienced. This has been symbolized by a row of matches that are burning each other until we remove just one match, *confining* it from the flames and breaking the cycle, providing a hope for something new. Confinement can serve as a safety barrier to stop the spread of viruses and fires, and confinement can prevent, or reduce the impact of, burnout.

Burnout

I know when I have hit a limit because I start to see stars in my eyes. I remember holding onto the desk at work when my colleagues were laughing with each other, and my boss was telling me that he was going for a coffee and that I should join him. There was no reason for it, but I started to panic, certain that he was taking me for a coffee to fire me.

It felt like my surroundings were closing in on me, and I thought I was going to pass out. It wasn't anything about my boss, or my job, but I knew I had been taking on too much since the pandemic. Gone were the boundaries of the working day, and I had been working through the night at some points. Stupid, I know, but I assumed everyone else was doing it, so I should too. As much as I knew how much I had been overdoing it, I knew what I needed, and that was time out. It didn't really matter what form that took, I just needed to be away from the constant questions about which type of portfolio we need to concentrate on, or what to promise which client, and whether we could deliver.

My boss could see something was up and, would you believe it, he just told me I could take the rest of the day off. In fact, he ordered me to, and when I tried to push back with worries about a couple of deals, he said he would handle it all until tomorrow.

I ended up just driving to some side road and staring at the cars swishing by. It was the best twenty minutes I've had in over two years.

- Tamara, 35 years old.

For some, burnout is seen as a badge of honor. They work to the point of collapse and claim that this proves that they have a *good work ethic*, or *strength*, and yet it is neither. In the case of Tamara, she was so exhausted that she was losing concentration every day she had to drive to or from work. "I didn't even realize I was falling asleep until something pulled at my attention," she once said. "Next thing I was aware of, I was swerving too hard, and I slammed into a tree. Thank goodness I was the only person injured."

Notwithstanding the risk to others, burnout can be damaging to your own health. Research shows that burnout can thin the gray matter of your prefrontal cortex (the part of your brain that is responsible for important functions such as reasoning and decision-making), and it can enlarge the amygdala (the brain's alarm system). As a result, when our alarm system goes into overdrive, we sense threat when there is none, and we are less able to mediate this heightened state with cool, calming reason. An amygdala in overdrive activates the sympathetic nervous system, our fight-or-flight response, which can lead to higher levels of stress hormones, including cortisol and epinephrine. Increased levels of epinephrine damage blood vessels and arteries and raise blood pressure, and excessive cortisol levels result in an increased fat tissue.

In the 1970s psychoanalyst Herbert J. Freudenberger was one of the first to conceptualize burnout, and there have been varying definitions since. In 2019, the World Health Organization classified burnout as an occupational phenomenon in the International Classification of Diseases (ICD-11). The American Psychological Association carried out a survey in 2021 and it revealed that "79% of employees had experienced work-related stress in the month before the survey." It also showed that "nearly 3 in 5 employees reported negative impacts of work-related stress" and 44% reported "physical fatigues—a 38% increase since 2019." The survey also revealed that some professions were more prone to burnout, notably teachers and healthcare workers. Although the World Health Organization limited the definition to workplace stress, you can see how features can be applied to other contexts. Burnout occurs when there is chronic stress that has not been successfully managed, and to borrow from the World Health Organization's definition, it is characterized by "feelings of energy depletion or exhaustion," "feelings of negativism or cynicism," and reduced "efficacy."

Arguably, we are at greater risk of burnout because we have confined ourselves from the rhythms of Mother Nature. No longer are we hunter-gatherers who train our attention minutely on the next kill to ensure our survival. Neither are we (in the words of Jon Kabat-Zinn, in *Meditation is Not What You Think*) farmers "naturally entrained into the rhythms of the earth." According to Kabat-Zinn, we have invented so many time-saving and labor-saving devices that we have become less dependent on Mother Nature, but also more isolated from natural rhythms. One of the prime suspects, according to Kabat-Zinn, is "the digital revolution" which has resulted in our continual bombardment "with texts, push notifications, appeals, deadlines, communications, and way too much information that we don't need and can't possibly take in and process." Hot on the heels of the growth in digital devices and other technology, burnout has been fueled by worsening environmental pollution, the threat of another world war, and the fallout from the COVID-19 pandemic. Even though restrictions are being lifted, we are still adjusting to a dramatically changed world.

Carlos was awoken by the angry roar of a distant leaf blower. Despite his exhaustion over the last two years, he could not remember the last time he fell asleep before the break of dawn. He dismissed his exhaustion as just part of the role as a business analyst in a Fortune 500 company, with a busy schedule and not much else going on in his life. As he opened the curtains to a flourish of yellow crocuses scattered throughout the flower bed, he longed for his college days, when he could savor each change in season. But he knew he had to make every day in his career count. His parents had never gone to college, so he carried the weight of their expectations like a millstone around his neck. He had plenty of annual leave to use up, but he refused to take it because he was determined to make an impression with his boss, Marcus, who barely acknowledged Carlos, offering curt one-syllable replies on the good days, and sighs or a shrug when he had less patience. The more Marcus rebuffed Carlos, the more he tried to impress his boss.

One spring evening, as the sun stretched across the Hudson, Carlos decided to go beyond Marcus's instructions and fill the gaps with what he believed to be initiative. It turned out, as he learned during a fiery meeting that followed, Carlos's *initiative* equated to borderline negligence. Under this stress, Carlos's amygdala became enlarged, the gray matter of his prefrontal cortex was thinned, and he was overwhelmed by a sense of hopelessness. Still he worked harder to impress his boss, and he slept and ate less, and the mistakes kept piling up. He stopped returning calls from his friends and family, and eventually his parents found him in his apartment after he failed to show up to work. He refused to leave his bed, and it seemed like he hadn't washed all weekend. Carlos was showing all the signs of burnout.

**

Respite – How to recognize the signs of burnout

Keep an eye out for the following signs of burnout. If you have any concerns, consult your doctor or therapist:

- Exhaustion
- Insomnia
- Helplessness
- Changes in your eating habits
- Anger
- Irritability
- Cynicism
- Reduced interest in things you usually enjoy
- An inability to think clearly
- Apathy
- An overwhelmingly negative outlook on life
- Breathlessness
- Reduced effectiveness with tasks
- Dizziness

**

Temporary confinement — A period for mental convalescence, and a fire barrier to prevent burnout

Notifications flash or bleep on our phone every second. The doorbell rings, our children are calling us, and our partner needs help with something. And we haven't even got to the overflowing inbox of work emails. We try to focus and yet we scroll through a series of banal comments on Twitter, or confusing videos on TikTok, and then we realize we need to start opening our work emails. And then the phone rings, and then we are hungry or need the bathroom, or we are again interrupted by our children.

Whether it is in the workplace or at home, we can avoid burnout by confining ourselves from constant demands on our attention. As Dr. Gavin Francis points out in *Recovery: The Lost Art of Convalescence*, "to flourish we have to build in moments of rest and reflection,"— and this is not a new concept made famous by Generation Z. Francis points to the Middle Ages, when people took pilgrimages for religious reasons but also to heal. As Chaucer wrote in *The Canterbury Tales, "And specially, from every shire's end Of England, to Canterbury they wend, The holy blissful Martyr for to seek, Who helped them when they were sick."* In *Quiet: The Power of Introverts in a World That Can't Stop Talking*, Susan Cain explains how important it is to take time out from the endless distractions and rest within the confines of some form of mental peace. "Solitude can be a catalyst to innovation," she claims. "Personal space is vital to creativity," she continues, and excessive stimulation in the form of open-plan offices can "reduce productivity and impair memory," raise heart rates, and increase cortisol levels. Excessive stimulation has also been found to impede the learning process, especially because, according to Cain, "scientists now know that the brain is incapable of paying attention to two things at the same time."

Convalescence doesn't have to be long periods of time, so Carlos does not have to resign from his much-sought-after career and set off on a pilgrimage to Canterbury. We can carve out small but regular periods of time when we rest from the constant demands of life. A moment of confinement, or a period for mental convalescence. Like creating a fire barrier, you can give yourself permission to take a break from achieving more, learning more, or earning more, just as much as you can step out of the anxiety-provoking fears of an uncertain future that burn your confidence and tell you that you are going to miss something or get caught unaware. You can tell yourself that, for this brief period, you are going to stop following those thoughts to their logical conclusion, and you are going to refuse to believe the heart-burning fluttering that stirs in your stomach. For a brief period of confinement, you do not need to keep fulfilling the expectations you or others have that you will be the cheerful one, or the thoughtful one, or the sociable or hardworking one. When my clients realize that they can give themselves this brief period of convalescence, their faces seem to soften, as if I have lifted the weight of expectation from their mind. Some clients even report that they feel less of the weight of the hangdog jowl of depression, where they have assumed, for too long, that they are smaller than they really are and any challenges to their life are far bigger and uglier than reality upholds.

To rest within your confines, to allow for a period of mental convalescence, can involve inactivity and the absence of stress, but it is far from a passive exercise. As Francis points out in *Recovery: The Lost Art of Convalescence*, convalescence is "an act, and actions need us to be present, to engage, to give of ourselves." During this period of mental convalescence, you need to confine yourself from the daily stressors that activate the fight-or-flight response of your sympathetic nervous system, the shutdown of the dorsal vagal response, or the *servitude and ingratiation* of the fawn response. You need to actively work on activating the ventral vagal response of your parasympathetic nervous system. Research shows that if you engage in daily meditation or mindfulness exercises, you can activate the ventral vagal response of your parasympathetic nervous system and see a reduction in harmful cortisol levels. There are plenty of meditation or mindfulness exercises available, and I have some on my website at www.chriswarrendickins.com.

Part of this active approach to confinement involves mindfulness. Mindfulness ensures that you remain active within this temporary period of convalescence because it keeps you alert to the present moment and all that makes up that moment, including your emotions, thoughts, and bodily sensations. Through mindfulness you become fully aware of the moment so you do not end up sleepwalking through life and trapping yourself within a prison of distraction, delusion, numbness, or overstimulation. Mindfulness has been overcomplicated over the years. In some respects, people have hijacked the concept, leaving others to (mistakenly) believe that you have to jump on a plane to a retreat in Colorado, or purchase an expensive training program to get to grips with a mindful approach to life. But mindfulness is a great deal more accessible (and affordable) than that. Mindfulness is simply the practice of letting go, or "non-doing," as Kabat-Zinn refers to it in his book *Full Catastrophe Living*, and you can engage in mindfulness when you participate in any part of your life. You can mindfully sit, walk, interact with your partner, make love to your partner, play a sport, listen to music, eat, fill the dishwasher, play with your kids, or help your kids with schoolwork or bedtime routines. Mindfulness should not be confused with a relaxation exercise because the intention behind relaxation is to achieve a different state than your currently agitated and stressed-out state—namely, to relax. In contrast, the purpose of a mindfulness exercise is to become aware of what *is*—even if that is agitated or stressed out—and not to change it. Instead, you are fully aware of the thoughts, emotions, and bodily sensations involved with that current state of agitation, and you are accepting them for the moment.

**

Respite – How to practice mindfulness

When it comes to periods of mental convalescence, confine yourself to some simple mindfulness exercises, such as the one set out below.

The more opportunities you have to practice mindfulness, the more you will benefit from it.

- Focus on your breathing to settle your attention into the present moment.
- If your mind starts to wander, don't judge yourself, because that is what minds are supposed to do. Just gently bring your attention back to your breathing.
- Notice any thoughts that come up and allow them to float away like bubbles. Don't try to change any thoughts or follow any to their logical conclusion. Just notice the thoughts from a distance. You can do this by saying silently to yourself *Ah yes, there is that thought, I see it,* and then redirecting your attention to your breathing.
- Each time you refocus on your breathing, you are creating a space between your thoughts and your reaction. Within this space you can make choices about how you respond.
- Notice any one-word emotions that might arise (anger, sadness, fear, loneliness), but, as with your thoughts, just notice those emotions without judgment. Don't try to change your emotions; say silently to yourself *Ah, yes, there is the anger/sadness/fear/loneliness,* and then redirect your attention to your breathing.
- As with your thoughts, you do not let those emotions hijack your awareness, and so by refocusing on your breathing, you are carving out more space between your emotions and your awareness. As with your thoughts, the more space you have between your

emotions and your awareness, the more choice you have about how to respond.

- Notice your bodily sensations. Sometimes your body serves as a bridge between your awareness and your emotions. Do you feel any discomfort, any tension, any softness, hardness, or anything else about your body? Don't try to change your bodily sensations, just notice them.
- As with your thoughts and emotions, don't try to change the bodily sensations but just notice them with *Ah yes, there is that sensation,* and then redirect your attention to your breathing.
- If you find it hard to focus on your breathing, focus on the subtle temperature change of your breath as it goes in through your nostrils, and out through your mouth. Some people find it useful to imagine a white ribbon going in through the nostrils, down the body, and then out through the mouth.
- Remember the key principles of mindfulness: Acceptance, awareness without judgment, and the practice of *non-doing* and *letting go* as described by Kabat-Zinn in *Full Catastrophe Living*. Mindfulness is not about relaxation. Mindfulness is about awareness and acceptance of your current state, and this includes acceptance of not being relaxed. Noticing your internal state at this level of awareness is the opposite of distraction, and the opposite of being "checked out" or dissociated from your body and mind.

**

It is a good idea to create a large portfolio of exercises so you have variety, because some will work better than others. The point of these periods of confinement is to afford yourself time to resist the urge to fight every good fight; to let yourself off the hook when it comes to every social gathering despite fear of missing out; to point to three examples of how you have already done well in your job—and in this job market, it is pretty easy to find a new job anyway; and to trust in your instincts that your kids are just fine with what knowledge and social skills they already possess, at least for now. Confinement in all these cases is about stepping back into your own comfort zone for a little, when you have tried to change things just a bit too much and have hit the point of exhaustion, or the point when you are achieving nothing but hitting your head against a brick wall.

Life is a balance, and one of the greatest gifts we can give ourselves is to learn when we need change and when we need stability, when we need to reach beyond our confines, beyond our comfort zone, and when we can let go and rest a little, confining ourselves to what we have now and accepting that this is enough. We can recognize the need for a period of confinement when we start to feel dizzy, when we start to lose interest in the things that usually fuel our passions, when we are overwhelmed with negativity—that is our body and mind telling us that we need to confine ourselves. When we have certain medical procedures we allow for a period of mental convalescence. In a similar way, we need recovery and healing of our mental health after we have endured challenging experiences, whether one or two major events (such as a pandemic with its series of variants) or a cumulation of personal adverse experiences.

Convalescence – a preserve of the privileged?

The Wellcome Collection is a museum and library dedicated to exhibits about health and well-being. I feel particularly connected to this museum because it sits amongst the beautiful old buildings of University College London, where I read law in the late 1990s. The museum displays a series on convalescence, including a print by Humphry Repton called *A View of the Parade at Bath*. In the southwest of England, Bath was where the wealthy spent long periods of convalescence, lured, according to the museum curators, by the belief that the water contained healing qualities. Of course, the poor could not afford such lavish indulgences, and instead of convalescing, they worked through their pain and discomfort. Adding to this illusive, *out of reach* nature, in *Recovery: The Lost Art of Convalescence*, Francis points out how surprising it is that words such as "convalescence are generally absent from the index of medical textbooks," making it seem even further out of reach. So is convalescence a preserve of the privileged?

My clients often tell me that they cannot find the time or inclination to engage in any periods of confinement, no matter how brief. For some reason, the idea of doing mindfulness or meditation exercises escapes their mind, or if they do think of it, they dismiss it as unimportant or too time-consuming. "I came to you because of burnout, because I am so overly scheduled that I haven't got time for a bathroom break, and you are adding more to my schedule?" I would understand their frustration if I had asked them to book into a mindfulness retreat for the next week, but all that is required for positive results is a matter of minutes each day—probably less time than it takes to get their morning coffee from their favorite café. Studies show that you can see improvements to your health when you spend around fifteen minutes engaging in some sort of mindfulness or meditation practice, provided you do this daily for around eight weeks. The more minutes you do, and the more weeks, the more you will see results, so start with a few minutes each day and try to build up to around fifteen minutes each day. It is worth noting, however, that the longer you have been living in a way that overly uses your sympathetic nervous system or triggers the shutdown of the dorsal vagal response of your parasympathetic nervous system, the longer it will take for this period of confinement to show beneficial results.

Before Carlos became a business analyst, he had spent a large proportion of his childhood living with his grandparents, having made the journey from Columbia on his own when he was just thirteen. When he spoke of those early years with his grandparents in a small town in Pennsylvania, his eyes grew dark and distant. "I know they didn't want me around," he would tell his friend. "They were past the age to keep up with a young kid, and to them I was just an inconvenience." "Nothing excuses the way they treated you," his friend would reply, even though he knew Carlos would find it hard to apportion any blame to his grandparents.

From the moment Carlos had arrived in Pennsylvania, his grandparents had beaten him with a belt, sometimes letting the metal buckle pierce his skin to leave open wounds—wounds that never received any medical treatment. And as Carlos preferred to be anywhere but within the four wood-paneled, cedar-smelling walls of his grandparents' home, the wounds would get infected during the hours he spent playing outside with other children.

In adulthood, Carlos was confused by some of his reactions to friendships, and his attempts to form relationships with women, never quite feeling anything for them. Finally, with the help of a therapist, he started to identify this as being stuck in a shutdown response of his dorsal vagal pathway. He also, at times, would see red and explode at a friend or work colleague, and in college he had got into trouble for punching holes in the walls of his dorm room. With the help of the therapist, he started to recognize this as the fight-or-flight response of his sympathetic nervous system, and he understood that these frequent outbursts of anger were inevitably increasing his cortisol levels (the stress hormone that can build up and cause so much damage to our health). As Carlos had experienced abuse at the hands of his grandparents for so many years, it would take a long time to notice the positive effects of any periods of mental convalescence in the form of mindfulness and meditation exercises. This is not to say that he would not benefit, and his cortisol levels would not reduce, it would just take time and space.

According to Dr Francis, when we attempt to heal, we become like "a gardener who sets out to 'grow.'" Any gardener knows that we need a combination of hard work, patience, and rest, just as the crop cycle includes a period of fallow to allow the soil to recover its nutrients. In *Recovery: The Lost Art of Convalescence* Francis cites Victoria Sweet, associate professor of medicine at the University of California, who claims that the tendency of hospitals to move patients quickly in and out of care has resulted in a neglect of "the value of slow recovery" and, indeed, any focus on a period of convalescence. We are not arguing for lavish trips to Bath but we do need a balance struck between the frantic pace and cost-effectiveness of today's life and the value of patience, healing, and calm.

Perhaps this is too much to ask for in such a fast-paced world, where the average amount of time to hold a person's attention on social media is the fifteen seconds of a TikTok video. Little is known about the long-term impact of rapidly evolving technology, but emerging research indicates that frequent use of digital technology can result in heightened attention-deficit symptoms, impaired emotional and social intelligence, technology addiction, social isolation, impaired brain development, and disrupted sleep. Some research does, however, indicate that there are some benefits. According to the paper "Brain Health Consequences of Digital Technology Use" there has been an increase "in brain neural activity during simulated internet searches" and "certain computer programs and videogames may improve memory, multitasking skills, fluid intelligence, and other cognitive abilities."

No matter the outcome of the research into these digital devices, we do need to keep an eye on our tendency to rush from one distraction to the next. Whether the distractions are work, family, or social media, we need to continuously assess how much time and energy is being taken by these distractions, and how much time and energy we are allocating for peace, healing, and a refocus on our internal strengths and resources. We often look for information and support from all life's distractions, forgetting that a wealth of knowledge and wisdom can be discovered within ourselves—endless information just waiting to be plundered. We just require a little time and space to explore our depths. *In Recovery: The Lost Art of Convalescence,* Francis explained that health is "the equilibrium between extremes, rather than an end in itself to be 'reached' or 'achieved.'" So too is the balance between reaching beyond and resting within our confines.

A period to rest within the confines of our natural introverted or extroverted state

A quiet secluded life in the country, with the possibility of being useful to people to whom it is easy to do good, and who are not accustomed to have it done to them; then work which one hopes may be of some use; then rest, nature, books, music, love for one's neighbor — such is my idea of happiness.

– Leo Tolstoy

Sounds great, doesn't it? I often think of this quotation when I am asked to speak about one of my books. I love sitting and writing, and I often enjoy talking to someone one-on-one, although I like the time-limited structure of the therapeutic hour. On the other hand, if you want me to stand on a stage in front a sea of faces, my legs start to shake.

Confinement works when we allow ourselves periods for convalescence, when we can rest within the confines of our natural rhythm, be that a state of introversion or of extroversion. The concept of introverts and extroverts was first introduced by Carl Jung in the 1920s. The terms have gained popularity over the years, and there are workplaces and universities that use tests (for example, the Myers-Briggs personality test) to identify the psychological types of their employees. In *Beyond the Blue*, I criticized the use of labels when it comes to human nature, because a label often overly simplifies our understanding of that person. And as we are a quick-natured species, forming fast opinions that are then generalized, we can start with a label and spin out as we objectify or pathologize that person, making assumptions and forming opinions that are based on half-baked knowledge that takes us far beyond the true sense of this person. The labels of "introvert" and "extrovert" are not immune to this criticism. However, some people take comfort from an ability to identify their own general tendency towards introversion or extroversion. It is one thing to use labels about other people, it is another to self-identify.

In *Quiet: The Power of Introverts in a World That Can't Stop Talking*, Susan Cain claims that you can distinguish introversion from extroversion by identifying the different "level of outside stimulation" that a person needs to function well. Introverts "feel 'just right' with less stimulation," and extroverts "enjoy the extra bang that comes from activities like meeting new people." Extroverts tend to derive more energy from social interaction, directing their energy outwards, whereas introverts direct their energy inwards and tend to feel drained around others. If you are inclined to be more extroverted, self-care can include giving yourself permission to leave the dishes in the sink and run out to meet the friends you have been missing. If you're more on the introverted side, this means you give yourself permission to rest at home and watch that Netflix series or read that backlog of books, as you have been promising yourself. Cain refers to the introversion-extroversion divide as a *spectrum* or *continuum* and says that our place on it affects every aspect of our lives, personal to professional. According to Cain, "one third to one half of Americans are introverts" (although she adds the caveat "depending on which study you consult"), and yet, she explains, American culture seems to reward extroversion, dismissing introversion "along with its cousins sensitivity, seriousness, and shyness" as "second-class" personality traits.

This has not always been so. Cain points to the 1920s, when there was a noticeable shift in the tone of self-help books. Self-help guides once helped people to identify a sense of "inner virtue," whereas from the 1920s there developed an emphasis on the importance of "outer charm." Cain believes that the development of industrial America contributed to the rise of extroversion as the American ideal. At this time the United States "quickly developed from an agricultural society of little houses on the prairie" to an urbanized, "'the business of America is business' powerhouse." Suddenly it was not enough to satisfy yourself with the close-knit community of people you had grown up with. If you were to survive in this fast-evolving powerhouse, you had to quickly learn how to push yourself forward and work with strangers. Americans had to learn how to "sell not only their company's latest gizmo but also themselves."

How clearly we see today this focus on outer charm. We are inundated by smiling, dazzling images on Instagram and TikTok that offer snapshots of what others want to project. How exhausting for people who lean more towards the introverted end of the spectrum—and even more reason for us to give ourselves permission to stop, take stock, and allow our body and mind to rest within our natural rhythms. In the same way that some chronically ill patients achieve a sense of peace when they finally have a diagnosis, knowledge of the limitations on our natural tendencies can help us achieve a sense of peace that will aid the process of mental convalescence. Rather than being pulled away by the next online or in-person distraction, you can pause to discover a "sense of entitlement to be yourself."

Our rubber-band tendencies

Once we have rested within the confines of our own natural tendencies, we will find there are times when we need to reach beyond those confines, beyond our comfort zone. But how much is that possible? If we are on the more introverted end of the spectrum, how realistic or fair is it to expect that we can try a different way of being? Can we, or indeed *should* we, fill up our weekends with coffees, lunches, and dinners with people we don't feel any natural inclination to catch up with? Should we keep volunteering for those work presentations that other people thrive on and seem to deliver without much in the way of preparation? This can have a significant impact on the direction of the one life we have, and the mental health we can enjoy or destroy.

Kim would often call her therapist in tears. No matter how many times she took a deep breath and stepped into a bar, she would end up standing alone as other people chatted enthusiastically with each other, or, more often than not, she would turn around and walk straight out without even catching one person's eye. Kim knew that she was naturally more inclined to spend quiet nights in on her own but her sister kept telling her that she needed to meet more people. Her sister had always enjoyed being around lots of people, and this left Kim feeling like she had to run to keep up with her energy.

In her book *Quiet*, Cain explores the work of Carl Schwartz, director of the developmental neuroimaging and psychopathology research laboratory at Massachusetts General Hospital. Schwartz proposes that we have "inborn temperaments" that "influence us, regardless of the lives we lead." At the same time, he says, we also have "*elasticity*" because we have "free will and can use it to shape our personalities." In other words, we have free will but we also have genetic limits. As Cain points out, "Bill Gates is never going to be Bill Clinton, and Bill Clinton can never be Bill Gates, no matter how much time he spends alone with a computer."

When Kim heard about this research, it gave her some comfort. She realized that she could try little strategies to regain confidence in social situations, including conserving her energy until right before a night out, using breathing and grounding exercises to center herself, and reminding herself of all her strengths and qualities. With a calmer mind, she realized there were some people in these bars who were equally uncomfortable, and who were actually quite interesting. For the infrequent times she forced herself out, she did end up having a reasonable time. At the same time, she kept her expectations realistic: she was never going to be a social butterfly, and she was comfortable with that.

Convalescence in the form of temporary periods of confinement are not just nice, they are essential. When you allow yourself space to breathe and grow, you activate the ventral vagal response of your parasympathetic nervous system so you can connect and heal. You prevent burnout, and you give yourself the chance to break the cycle of adverse childhood experiences. Once you have rested, you can face the world again, and you can see the world as it is rather than a distortion that creates fears and anxiety.

What creates the greatest distortion of how we perceive life? What keeps us in the darkest depths of that Internal Prison? Surely it is a fear that goes right to our core, the nightmare that haunted our predecessors even before they could stand upright, and well before our knack for invention accelerated at the speed of light. From the very beginning, shadows of *uncertainty* have terrified us because they pose an unquantifiable threat. What we do not know we cannot prepare for, and we, as a species, hate to *not know*.

But the shadows might hold hope as much as fear. If we can shed light on what tricks we play to trap our minds from within, and what falsehoods we tell ourselves late into the night, we might learn something. If we look a little closer, we might spot the coin hidden in the side of the top hat, or the trap door where the woman escapes without getting sawn in half. We can see our mental tricks for what they are: a labyrinthian prison of our own creation.

How are you confined by an intolerance of uncertainty?

CHAPTER 3

Confined by an intolerance of uncertainty

Uncertainty is an uncomfortable position.
But certainty is an absurd one.
- Voltaire

I can't handle this constant rollercoaster. If it isn't the exams, it is the choice of college, and if it isn't that it is whether or not my girlfriend is going to stay with me, and if it isn't that, it is . . ."

At this point, Jack burst into a wail that surprised the both of us. This was the most I had seen of his face, since so much of our time spent previously had involved a view of the top of his head, which tended to hang down over his iPhone. Sixteen-year-old Jack was in therapy on the orders of his concerned parents, which is the way most teenagers find their way into a therapist's office. Often when it is the parents who put the teen in therapy, the early part of our work can be characterized by one-word answers. That's how it had been in my work with Jack—until the moment it all tumbled out of him.

When his parents first spoke to me, they described his complaints about a pounding heart, sweat, and racing thoughts that plowed through multiple scenarios of potential threats to his well-being. According to his pediatrician, his physical health was fine, and so the pediatrician and Jack's parents labeled him a "worrier," thus extinguishing any further curiosity about his behavior and mood. I have already mentioned how labels can obscure the complexity of a problem, and they rarely offer a sufficient explanation for human behavior. Jack's issue wasn't the exams, or the choice of college, or the latest girlfriend. Jack had an intolerance for uncertainty. When I shared this with him, he nodded in agreement. "It is always the same," he sighed into the air that had thickened between us. "As soon as I get over one issue, as soon as the exams are over, or I get a good grade, or my friends are okay with me again, I am back onto the next issue, whether that is why my girlfriend hasn't responded to my messages, or whether my parents and I are going to be able to afford to get through college."

As Voltaire explains, "uncertainty is an uncomfortable position," but to reject it, to pretend that we can somehow avoid it or live a life of certainty, is an "absurd" position, and likely to keep us trapped inside an Internal Prison. And the irony was not lost on Jack when he referred back to the "worrier" label that his parents and the pediatrician had reached for. He could see that by doing that, his parents and pediatrician were perhaps trying to manage their own intolerance of uncertainty.

We are not built to favor uncertainty. Imagine what it was like for hunter-gatherers who experienced uncertainty as life threatening. In the face of uncertainty, they ran the risk of starving to death, or not finding a warm, dry shelter. Gone are those days, at least for many people, but, if we are not careful, our brain can end up perceiving any uncertainty with the same sense of visceral threat to life as our hunter-gatherer predecessors, and we can develop an anxiety disorder.

Not all anxiety is based on an intolerance of uncertainty, but it makes up a significant part. You can recognize anxiety if you constantly worry or ruminate, and people usually define anxiety as disproportionate fear, usually of something that might happen in the future. According to author Arthur Somers Roche, "anxiety is a thin stream of fear trickling through the mind. If encouraged, it cuts a channel into which all other thoughts are drained." Anxiety can be fueled by a tendency to *catastrophize*, which means you assume the worst about a potential threat and underestimate your ability to handle that threat. You might, for example, believe that you will make a mistake at work and lose your job, or you believe that you will run someone over if you drive home. There is no end to the list of ways to catastrophize.

The pandemic seems to have cracked open what certainty we might have once believed in. Just the fact of an airborne virus circulating without our having any real knowledge, initially, about its potency or lethality is uncertainty enough. Now we have some knowledge and vaccines, and we are emerging from confinement, blinking into the daylight like prisoners let out on early release. But there seems to be no "normal" to return to. Our cities have transformed, there are new variants of COVID, and the worlds of work and education seem to have permanently changed. So much that we once pointed to as *certain* and *knowable* has been called into question, so is it any wonder that there has been an increase in anxiety disorders? Since the pandemic, anxiety (and depression) have risen from one in ten adults to four in ten adults, and more people are reporting problems with eating, sleeping, and an increase in alcohol and substance use.

One explanation for the increase in anxiety is the different forms of loss that people endured. The pandemic wiped out families, and the long-term health of some survivors remains a huge burden. The pandemic also created significant losses in terms of livelihood, through job loss and business closures. This can all produce a significant sense of instability, and with that instability comes heightened vigilance; we are constantly alert for the next threat in this ever-more uncertain world.

The pandemic also created an increase in isolation. Isolation is particularly damaging when you are already struggling with challenges to your mental health, as these challenges in themselves can feel isolating.

Free to breathe

Tommy was at the doctor again for high blood pressure. For the last two years he had worked furiously to impress his new boss, and yet he was given yet another average score at his latest performance review. His wife had lost her job during the pandemic, and so it was down to him alone to support the family. They had just had a second child; and their eldest was struggling with school due to the interruptions during the pandemic, so Tommy was paying for a tutor as well. He felt trapped, but he had no option but to keep working harder, even though he could see no way to improve. Some of his peers had been promoted above him which really rubbed salt in the wound. Each night his mind raced over deals he had made, the way he had phrased emails with his boss and colleagues, and he could not find any answers. He was fighting against the uncertainty of his future at the company, the uncertainty about whether his wife would ever find another job, and the future of his eldest child's education. His exhaustion due to lack of sleep was destined to only make things worse.

According to Polyvagal Theory, uncertainty can quickly overwhelm the nervous system, so it is important to do anything to bring that person back up the nervous system ladder, out of the dorsal vagal state, or the sympathetic nervous system state, and into a ventral vagal state (the *social engagement system*). When you are in the ventral vagal state, Porges explains, you are much more able to lean in to and accept the uncertainty in your life than when you are in the dorsal ventral vagal state (shutdown), or in the fight-or-flight state of the sympathetic nervous system. However, when Tommy's doctor suggested mindful breathing exercises, he sneered. "So my career is going to be transformed by breathing. Nice one."

Tommy was not this doctor's first patient to doubt the effectiveness of breathing as a therapeutic strategy. Breathing is not the whole of the therapeutic work, but it is a useful starting point. Research shows that breathing exercises can help with anxiety and numerous other challenges to our mental health, including depression and post-traumatic stress disorder (PTSD). There are various ideas as to why. From a polyvagal perspective, you only need to think of the location of our *social engagement system*, the ventral vagal pathway, to understand the significance of breathing exercises. The vagus nerve runs from the stomach and diaphragm, up through the lungs and heart, and to the brain stem at the base of the skull, so when you change your breathing, you change (in the words of Stephen W. Porges in his book *The Polyvagal Theory*) the "tone of the autonomic nervous system." In *The Polyvagal Theory in Therapy,* Dana explains that when we change our breathing, "we engage the vagal pathways that influence the beating of the heart and the messages sent to the brain." The ventral vagal pathway, or *social engagement system*, is in our parasympathetic nervous system, so the more we can activate that, the better. Once we influence our autonomic response, we have greater freedom to influence our emotions and thoughts.

Mindfully focusing on our breathing can create a life buoy in a sea of uncertainty. Too often our mind gets hijacked by fears of a future uncertain and we become lost to the present moment. Focusing on our breathing puts us in the present moment, the one place we truly know about, and where we have a better chance of finding awareness and acceptance of what is actually happening rather than the distorted version of reality that we created due to our fears of uncertainty. Focusing on your breathing gives you a sense of *presence,* and this is helped when you use a compassionate voice to ask yourself "How are you doing with this uncertainty?" Whatever answer you get, reply "It is okay, you are doing the best you can." Presence is helped immensely when we focus on the moment without distractions. This is exceptionally hard—especially if our children, friends, or colleagues are all jostling for our attention—but the more we can turn off from our kids, work, social media, and friends, even for a moment, the more we are likely to gather a sense of presence and a stronger footing in the face of uncertainty.

Tommy tried to establish a sense of presence but instead of a compassionate inner voice, he found a harsh internal critic who found fault in the way he was doing the exercise, the way he was dressed, and the way he spoke. The doctor learned that this inner critic had been created during a childhood terrorized by a tyrannical father. Tommy's father would punish him for minor transgressions like coughing too loudly or leaving a light switch on, and his father found fault in everything about his son. It became clear to the doctor why Tommy had created such a hard outer shell, it had been necessary to survive the wrath of his father.

But life is not just about survival. Tommy survived at a cost to his ability to thrive. Like war veterans who flinch at the sound of loud bangs, Tommy was still nervous and easily startled. In other words, his sympathetic nervous system was often in a state of hyperarousal. When his eldest child slammed a door or dropped his schoolbag, Tommy's wife would point out how his fists clenched, and yet Tommy was not even aware that he was doing this. His amygdala, the brain's alarm system, was constantly alerting him to dangers that were not there, reducing the likelihood that he was able to use his prefrontal cortex for rational thought to mediate the storm. This was exhausting for him and everyone around him. Uncertainty can poke old wounds and dysregulate emotions, and it can disrupt our thought patterns. When we have survived adverse childhoods, we are more likely to imprison ourselves in all-or-nothing thinking. Although this black-and-white thinking gives us a false sense of certainty, it overly simplifies life, cutting out subtle shades of gray that might otherwise offer the hope of a more balanced perspective. Tommy's performance at work was not *all* bad, any more than his relationship with his boss was *all* a disaster. He had areas of strength and areas to improve. Tommy had more work to do to free himself of imprisoning thought patterns, but slowly, at least, his doctor was helping him to replace the words of his inner critic with a more compassionate voice. A big key to reaching beyond the confines of his adverse childhood was realizing that much of his process was understandable, given the circumstances, and he wasn't alone. We can all slip into these mental prisons, not least our intolerance of uncertainty.

**

Respite – Spot the signs of an intolerance of uncertainty

Trapped within your Internal Prison of an intolerance of uncertainty, you are likely to notice the following symptoms:

- Constant worry about the future
- Overplanning
- Irritability
- Easily startled
- A tendency to get overwhelmed when plans change
- An aversion to surprises
- Trouble getting to sleep and/or staying asleep
- Gastrointestinal issues, including diarrhea or constipation
- Restlessness, so your body is constantly moving (for example, your feet keep tapping or your legs or arms shake)
- Stiff shoulders and neck
- Headaches
- A tendency to undereat or overeat

**

Jack's parents were right to intervene when they did and get the professional help he needed because there are an infinite number of uncertainties in life, so the issue is not to create certainty. This is a form of avoidance, and avoidance tends to only fuel anxiety. Instead, with the help of a trained professional and his parents, Jack had to establish the same sense of presence that we outlined for Tommy. In addition, both Jack and Tommy needed to learn how to regulate their emotions in the face of uncertainty; I like to explain this as akin to riding a wave. We know that our anxiety might build up and peak with a cumulation of feelings, but if we stay with it, mindfully breathing through the experience, those feelings will subside. As a result, the brain does not fear the uncertainty the next time, or we do not fear it as intensely, because we have created new neural pathways, a new experience of the uncertainty. We experienced the peak of fear in the face of uncertainty, but also the diminishment of the feelings as the wave ebbed. We survived.

The value of a black swan of uncertainty

As mathematical statistician Nassim Nicholas Taleb wrote in *The Black Swan: The Impact of the Highly Improbable*, a black swan is an event that is an "outlier, as it lies outside the realm of regular expectations," which creates "an extreme impact." We try to explain its occurrence after the fact, "making it explainable and predictable." We think we *know* so much that we claim to explain the unexplainable. Quite the arrogant species are we Homo sapiens. Taleb claims that scientists and economists operate "under the false belief that their tools could measure uncertainty," and so we are blinded to randomness. When we are blind, we cannot learn, and so we remain—at least in this respect—unevolved. So we are not so great a species after all. To illustrate this, Taleb points to the attacks on September 11, 2001. If we had not been so blind to randomness and uncertainty, if we had not been so arrogant as to assume that we *know* so much, then maybe "fighter planes would have circled the sky above the twin towers" and "airplanes would have had locked bulletproof doors."

What the black swan shows us is that, at least in some contexts, we can harness the utility of uncertainty for our own benefit. Artists, musicians, writers, and actors use uncertainty to inspire masterpieces, top ten tunes, epic novels, and Broadway hits. William Godwin wrote that, "Hope is in some respects a thing more brilliant, more vivifying, than fruition.

What we have looked forward to with eager and earnest aspiration is never in all respects equal to the picture we had formed of it. The very uncertainty enhances the enjoyment."

We can learn from randomness and uncertainty as long as we can tolerate our anxieties about them. If we could reach beyond our Internal Prison of intolerance of uncertainty, we might be able to recognize the value of seeing how much we *do not know*. Then we might be able to learn. I have practiced as a lawyer and as a psychotherapist, and in both cases, it tends to be the clients who are willing to accept that they do not know everything who have the greatest hope of remaining out of prisons (of their own creation or actual prisons). Our children don't go into school with their hands over their ears, telling the teacher that they know it all already. We grow when we adopt a sense of curiosity, when we are flexible in our views so we can always hold space for new knowledge to make a home in our brain. In the same way we do not expect to see a black swan, our fear of uncertainty blinds us to the full range of possibilities that life presents for us. Accepting that we do not know as much as we think can provoke anxiety. If there are black swans, what else is lingering in the shadows outside the realms of our expectations? The integrity of our mind? The safety of our caregivers? The trust that we will be paid by our employers? The safety of our house at night?

Taleb claims that we are not just afraid of this uncertainty but, "we scorn the abstract." I find this in my work as a psychotherapist, when people turn to me to provide clearly defined (and comprehensive) answers to human equations of love, desire, loss, and despair. Sometimes the diagnostic label gives them this comfort of certainty, at least for a while, until they realize that many mental health conditions do not fit so neatly within such labels. As a result, the therapists who adopt a manualized approach, convinced that there is a treatment plan for every issue, and that all people will respond favorably to this finite list of interventions to be applied like spells chanted round a cauldron, will convince some people that they have *the answer*. And perhaps that placebo of certainty is enough for some. But for many—the majority, perhaps—the unavoidable truth is that interventions and effectiveness are as changeable in their effectiveness as quicksand, and sometimes only blind luck produces a favorable result. We, as therapists, bear the brunt of this truth, and the aversion people have for it. In *The Gift of Therapy*, Irvin D. Yalom claims that diagnosis tends to be helpful only in a small number of cases. Yalom explains that "psychotherapy consists of a gradual unfolding process wherein the therapist attempts to know the patient as fully as possible," whereas "a diagnosis limits vision; it diminishes ability to relate to the other as a person."

When George started therapy, he insisted that he was not the one who needed therapy. He had been getting into fights with his husband and, during their first session together, he said that his husband should be in therapy, not him.

"That may be true. Couples therapy is also an option," the therapist said with a smile.

"You'll never get him to agree," George responded, shrugging.

"So that just leaves you and I. Shall we see if there is anything we can accomplish together?"

"If you like."

It can be hard to start work when someone does not believe in therapy—especially when they believe the wrong person is there. There must be at least a small part of that person who is willing, or even a little bit curious, to see if anything can be gained. At first this therapist wondered whether there was even this small amount of willingness in George. He had heard the commotion George had made in the waiting room as he paced about and kicked the trash can with contempt. And when the therapist ventured out to greet him, George seemed to increase in size as his shoulders and arms spread open. He was stretching his relatively small, stocky frame to its furthest reach, and the therapist guessed that this might be more of an attempt at intimidation than a display of prowess.

At first George refused to answer any of the therapist's questions, so they kept things light and discussed anything but why George had come for therapy. When George could see that he had some sort of control over the process, that therapy was far from a medical procedure to be *done to him*, like the removal of a cancerous tumor, he seemed to trust a little more in the therapist. Eventually they got to the heart of why George had come to therapy, and that was because of his love for his husband.

"I can't lose him," he suddenly blurted out.

"Why might you lose him?"

"We have been fighting."

"Couples fight."

"I mean, bad fights. I can't lose him; he is the one good thing in my life."

"I hear you."

Over the course of their work together, the therapist could determine that George's marriage was at breaking point because of his outbursts of anger. A couple of times, when they had been out for dinner with their friends, they had got close to a fistfight. Finally, his husband, Paul, gave George an ultimatum: Therapy or divorce.

Although this was George's first experience as an adult in therapy, he had seen a psychiatrist when he was fourteen. The psychiatrist met with George a handful of times and slapped a diagnostic label of oppositional defiant disorder (ODD) on George's behavior, prescribing medication without much else in terms of support or investigation. Clearly that psychiatrist lacked the curiosity to try and discover *why* George had been acting in such a way. He seemed content to accept that he had identified George as a *white swan*, and that was that.

Twenty years later, with a wealth of knowledge about trauma, George's new therapist was more comfortable with a sense of uncertainty. People often act in certain ways for very good reasons. If we apply the Polyvagal Theory, we can act with anger and aggression when we feel unsafe. We are doing what we are supposed to do in deploying the fight-or-flight response of our sympathetic nervous system. Because any sense of safety is beyond our immediate perception—it is a threat we *neurocept*—no amount of explanation will help us to stand down our guard.

Because of this therapist's acceptance of not knowing—not knowing everything about George, but also not knowing everything about life and gender assumptions—there was space for George to share that as a child he had experienced years of sexual abuse at the hands of his mother. When it started, his father was working overseas, and his sister had moved out with her boyfriend.

George's words fell out of his mouth so softly that he probably thought they would be unheard. Like an orchid shedding its petals, all beauty was lost. In its place there stood an image of baron exposure. "She must have felt lonely and neglected" George muttered, attempting to explain away his mother's behavior. "She had no one else to turn to."

This explained a great deal about George's unruly behavior at school, and his anger ever since. Our intolerance of uncertainty means we fill the gaps where we should wait and see, and it is our intolerance of uncertainty that makes it hard to accept the black swans of male-labeled survivors of sexual abuse at the hands of female-labeled perpetrators.

Overtelling the story

Our intolerance of uncertainty really causes problems when it makes us construct stories that are tantamount to fairy stories when compared with our lived experiences. I am not referring to the kind of storytelling that your five-year-old engages in when they insist that it was really (*no, really, honestly, cross my heart and hope to die*) their newborn sister who wrote on the walls (and if this isn't accepted, then it was the cat, the goldfish, or the mailperson). I am referring to what Taleb calls *narrative fallacy*, or in other words, "our limited ability to look at sequences of facts without weaving an explanation into them." When we do this, we often use our emotions rather than the cortical part of the brain. Taleb argues that this tendency to create a narrative results in an illusion of certainty that might make us feel better but ends up distracting us from a deeper understanding of the problem. "Our propensity to impose meaning and concepts blocks our awareness of the details making up the concept," he wrote.

Our need to impose meaning or structure on the unknown is quite understandable once we start to drill in a little deeper. Studies show that "pattern perception increases along with the concentration in the brain of the chemical dopamine." So, when we fill in the gaps and create stories out of those blank spaces, we get a hit of our good friend the feel-good drug (dopamine), and we don't even have to pay a dealer. Who would pass up the chance? The trouble is, we end up missing some of the vital lessons that could be learned. Taleb claims that to avoid the errors of the narrative fallacy is to remember our brain's capacity to think rather than letting our emotions control us. We need to use the thinking part of our brain a bit more "to favor experimentation over storytelling, experience over history, and clinical knowledge over theories."

The Hero Expert as a Rescuer . . . or Confidence Artist?

Sometimes the narrative we tell ourselves involves a hero, as all great fables do. When we create this narrative, we hope for someone who is going to absolve us of the need to think for ourselves and, most importantly, to rescue us from intolerable uncertainty. But by doing this, what are we telling ourselves about our own ability to handle uncertainty? Are we viewing ourselves as a helpless *Victim* who needs a *Rescuer* to save us from the *Persecutor* that is uncertainty? Stephen Karpman first conceptualized this dynamic of social interaction, and he called it the *Drama Triangle*. This is a simple way to understand how we distort how we view our social interactions, creating a Victim, Rescuer, or Persecutor out of the people involved. When we view people, including ourselves, in terms of one of these three dramatic roles, we oversimplify our interactions, and we often end up with false hopes or crushing disappointment. For example, if we view ourselves as the helpless Victim, we might overlook our strengths and our own ability to rescue, or become the hero for, ourselves. When we view someone else as the Rescuer, we can attribute too much credit to this expert, leading to overreliance on this apparent Rescuer expert.

During his years at school, Dan had been the target of bullying by students who were two grades above him. In adulthood he was constantly alert for any signs of an abuse of power. No matter the context—at work with his colleagues or outside of work—he saw himself as the Rescuer for every perceived Victim of any perceived Persecutor. What he didn't appreciate was that this was an oversimplification of events, distorted by his own experiences of bullying, and so he overlooked the resources and strengths these apparent Victims may have possessed. He also overlooked any imbalance in power that existed to the disadvantage of the apparent Persecutor, and he overestimated his own ability to step in and become the Rescuer. Stuck in this Drama Triangle and staying up late every night trying to fight what he believed to be the "good fight," he was in danger of burnout. What Dan needed to appreciate was that he would be of no use to any crusades—even those where he could play a part in achieving some good—if he was burnt-out.

Dan could have fallen foul of Karpman's Drama Triangle in a different way if he had turned to a therapist or friend and viewed them as his Rescuer, thereby viewing himself as the Victim and the bullies the Perpetrators. If this had happened, Dan might have overlooked some of his own strengths and resources, viewing himself as disproportionately vulnerable and perhaps making himself more prone to anxiety or depression.

When you start to rely too much on a Rescuer, you run the risk of exposing yourself to people who take advantage of the

Drama Triangle. For some, your hope and vulnerability are an opportunity for gain, as Maria Konnikova explained in *The Confidence* Game, a book about confidence artists. She explains that the "Ponzi schemer," the "politician," the "healer," and the "religious leader," all turn up with the perfect solution to the problem of the moment, fitting neatly into the Drama Triangle as the archetypal Rescuer. I would add to that list the untrained, inexperienced, or unethical therapists, coaches, and other healthcare "professionals" who appear just when you believe that you can find no way out of your mental health challenges. Along with the other confidence artists, they deal in that addictive drug called *hope,* and some even offer the illusion of certainty. They were in high demand during the pandemic, and as Konnikova explains, confidence artists thrive "in times of transition and fast change, when new things are happening and old ways of looking at the world no longer suffice."

We cannot learn from uncertainty if we lean too heavily on supposed experts, a warning I expressed in *Beyond the Blue.* When I became a psychotherapist, I found that some clients would look to me as some sort of oracle, clinging to my every word as if I could somehow solve all their problems. And I had colleagues who believed in such hype. They would dance around client issues, throwing this technique and that, and it would often turn out to be a load of smoke and mirrors (for a very high price). What *Beyond the Blue* offered instead was an opportunity for readers to learn about certain mental health challenges, to check out whether any of it resonated with their own experiences. *Beyond the Blue* was not an *expert piece*, claiming to *know it all,* but instead an invitation *for* people to keep nimble on their own two feet in case they encountered their own version of an "outlier that has an extreme impact," as described in *The Black Swan.* I wanted to open people's minds to the possibility that certain "solutions" are far from panaceas and help them see that this open-mindedness can put them in a better position to handle the dark shadow of that black swan of uncertainty that can often throw things into chaos.

**

Respite – Signs you have become a Rescuer, Victim, or Persecutor

Signs that you have become a Rescuer:

- You are quick to jump in and try to solve other people's problems
- You become frustrated when people don't follow your advice
- You have a need to know everything about other people's lives
- People tend to turn to you for answers to their problems

Signs that you have become a Victim:

- You tend to rely more on someone else than on yourself to resolve your problems
- You are quick to blame other people
- You overly share details of your life with others, in the hope that you will be helped
- You tend to view yourself as helpless or vulnerable

Signs you have become a Persecutor:

- You tend to get the blame when things go wrong
- You are dismissed as "oversensitive" or an "unnecessary worrier"
- You identify yourself, or hear others refer to you as, the *scapegoat* of a group, whether that is by your own family, a group of friends, or a group of coworkers
- You are referred to as "the troublemaker"

**

Extreme uncertainty

Our intolerance of uncertainty can leave us clutching at any form of certainty. Research shows that the certainty offered by fundamentalist religions, extreme political groups, radical interest groups, and conspiracy theories promises a tempting relief to our anxiety. Part of us knows what is being promised is not the whole truth because it is so polished and over-simplified, but it is preferable to claim to *know* rather than admit that, for a great deal of life, we *cannot know*. Extremism also offers a sense of identity, a clear template so we do not have to struggle with what can sometimes be an uncomfortable process of self-discovery. As psychology professor Arie W. Kruglanski points out, one of the appealing factors is the "ideological narrative—the story a terrorist group tells to justify its actions," justifying the actions according to "group values."

Extremism has been around for a long time, but some argue that digital devices, the growth in technology, and social media have compounded things. According to the "United Nations Handbook on Children Recruited and Exploited by Terrorist and Violent Extremist Groups," one of the main strategies used to recruit children is the internet. Given the limited options to monitor children's use of online resources, this is particularly troubling. But is the growth in technology really a significant factor when it comes to extremism? After all, extremism has been fueled by the structural inequality and privilege that exists in countries such as the United States, not least because of the widening gap between the rich and poor. We only have to see how hard the pandemic hit certain communities and benefited others. At the very least, our digital devices can help us with awareness about the extent of extremism that some are turning to. Who can forget the red-faced, pot-bellied, angry white men who stormed the Capitol on January 6, 2021, incited by their extremist (and equally red-faced and pot-bellied) commander in chief? Who can forget their indignance as they shook their sweaty fists like entitled toddlers throwing a tantrum? It was a fertile time for extremism, coming hot on the heels of a pandemic, and as Ervin Staub points out in *The Roots of Evil: The Psychological and Cultural Origins of Genocide and Other Forms of Group Violence*, acts of extremism such as genocides "often arise under conditions of acute societal uncertainty."

In *The Confidence Game* Konnikova explains that we have a "need to believe in something that gives life meaning, something that reaffirms our view of ourselves, the world, and our place in it." We can see telltale signs in some of the people who end up gravitating towards extremism. For example, the disaffected sons of redundant Rust Belt workers, sunken into powerlessness, often end up gravitating towards extremist behavior. Certain groups offer them the hope of power (no matter how illusory that power may turn out to be). This highlights a wider problem in which cisgender, straight, white male-labeled people have the false belief that they are entitled to greater power than others should enjoy, thereby reacting with violence and aggression in the face of the reality that they do not deserve any more power than anyone else. According to physician Gabor Maté, writing in *When the Body Says No: The Cost of Hidden Stress*, "strong convictions do not necessarily signal a powerful sense of self: very often quite the opposite. Intensely held beliefs may be no more than a person's unconscious effort to build a sense of self to fill what, underneath, is experienced as a vacuum."

The ultimate uncertainty – a matter of perspective

For some, the ultimate uncertainty that cannot be tolerated is death. According to Yalom in *The Gift of Therapy*, "one of our chief modes of death denial is a belief in personal *specialness*, a conviction that we are exempt from biological necessity and that life will not deal with us in the same harsh way it deals with everyone else."

When I have worked with people who have faced death—their own or a loved one's—I notice how we turn inwards instead of rushing away from the various components of it. It feels like we are paying respects to the reality of this great unknown, bowing our heads with reverence to something that we finally cannot *know*, no matter what else we may claim to *know*. For some, I see a huge sense of relief in the dropping of the shoulders. Finally, no more fighting, no more working so hard to keep up with everything and to make sense of it all. It just is.

According to hospice and palliative medicine physician BJ Miller, most people do not fear being dead, but the process of dying or the possibility of suffering. During his sophomore year at Princeton, Miller was electrocuted after he climbed on top of a parked train, leaving him without both legs and half of one arm. As a result, he is well placed to opine on experiences of uncertainty, including near-death experiences. From those experiences, Miller learned that there is a fundamental distinction between "necessary and unnecessary suffering." To avoid unnecessary suffering, he says, "how we die is indeed something we can affect."

When a resident dies at the Zen Caregiving Project, a hospice in San Francisco where BJ Miller works, everyone stops work to sprinkle the body with flower petals as people share stories about the person who has passed, or they can just stand in a silent tribute; the choice is theirs. "It takes a few minutes," Miller says. "It's a sweet, simple parting image to usher in grief with warmth rather than repugnance." It is, he says, "perspective, that kind of alchemy we humans get to play with, turning anguish into a flower." How freeing is this image of our view of uncertainty—that with a change in perspective, we can transform it into something that is not a confining prison but as beautiful as anguish transformed into flower petals.

It can be hard to see the beauty of a flower, let alone a transformed perspective, when we are trapped inside a prison of our own creation. Cool, dark corners of perceived limitations and inadequacies can drain the color out of life as quickly as you lose a sense of hope or meaning. When we are trapped by depression and low self-esteem, we are weakened from the inside, just as a building is undermined by a crumbling foundation.

How are you confined by an Internal Prison of depression and low self-esteem?

CHAPTER 4

Confined by depression and low self-esteem

Depression is a prison where you are both the suffering prisoner and the cruel jailer.
- Dorothy Rowe

Many of the mandates have been lifted, and we can attend a gym again, and our children are even at an in-person school rather than a Google Meet class. And yet some of us are still locked in an Internal Prison of depression and low self-esteem. It isn't as if the pandemic created these challenges to mental health, but the situation was made a great deal worse because of it, not least because access to mental health care has worsened since the pandemic. According to recent reports, four in ten adults in the US reported depression (or anxiety), an increase from one in ten in 2019. This is not surprising, given the impact COVID had on job losses, a lack of opportunity to socialize (leading to isolation), and a sense of powerlessness that an unknown virus created.

Depression is characterized by a low mood, an over-estimation of the negativity of life circumstances, and an under-estimation of our capability to handle challenges. We feel hopeless and powerless, and often we cannot point to a specific reason for this overwhelmingly negative outlook. People will assume that they have failed completely at life, and there is no way out of this, or they will be unable to see any point in reaching out for support, even if those options for support occur to them. As C.S. Lewis put it in *The Problem of*

Pain, "It is easier to say 'My tooth is aching' than to say 'My heart is broken.'" With this bleak picture in mind, it is clear to see why depression and suicide is closely related. The worst moments of depression are when you cannot point to any root cause, any crashing loss or catastrophe to cause so much pain. It is a dull pain that lingers, and it discolors everything that you see. It weighs you down with hopelessness like a wet rubber blanket, and no matter how hard you shake it, still it clings to you like dread.

The trouble with depression is that it can adopt many different guises, and so, for some, it can push them into over-eating, over-exercising, or over-working, whereas others lose their appetite, or retreat to their bed, or start to drink alcohol again. Some people report a blank mind, or a heaviness to the body, others notice a sharp uptick of anger and irritability. However, one characteristic seems to prevail over all symptoms, and that is a sense of inescapability from it. This isn't the mental health Olympics, but at least with something like OCD, if you do go through the routine (touch the table four times, say the magic words in the correct way), you get some sort of relief. Depression stays, solidifying your feet like tombs of cement. There is no escape.

Playing dead to survive

According to Polyvagal Theory, the symptoms of depression can be viewed as the dorsal vagal response of the parasympathetic nervous system, the most primitive, or the bottom of the evolutionary "ladder." We become immobilized or shutdown. If you think of someone being threatened in their home, with words or actions, if they respond with an adrenalin-fueled fight, standing up to the aggressor, this might expose them to a greater risk of harm, especially if the victim is a child being threatened by an overbearing adult. Viewed in this way, the shutdown immobilization response of depression seems quite smart if you want to survive (*The Polyvagal Theory*, Stephen W. Porges). Linked to this *immobilization* are two common symptoms of depression, and that is a sense of shame, and a sense of hopelessness, and these symptoms can isolate us further, leaving us trapped within the confines of our own sense of inadequacy. However, when we start to understand that depression can be a survival strategy, this can alleviate the shame and hopelessness, freeing us to reach beyond our confines and connect with others, a process of co-regulation that reinforces the healing steps out of depression.

Sometimes when I start work with a depressed client, they express a belief that their depression will be eradicated if only they can work hard enough. They have bought books, and they attended courses, and they keep to an exercise regime in the belief that all of this will prevent them from feeling as badly as they once did. The reality is that depression can linger in the background, becoming more or less intense as time goes on. This was perfectly described by Sylvia Plath in *The Bell Jar* when she wrote, "Wherever I sat—on the deck of a ship or a street cafe in Paris or Bangkok—I would be sitting under the same glass bell jar, stewing in my own sour air." You can use certain strategies and skills to lessen the impact, but it is unrealistic to expect that you will never be touched by depression again. Just as hard to accept is the fact that the presence or absence of depression can seem arbitrary. All at once, for no apparent reason, depression rears its ugly head, and then, for no identifiable reason, it disappears again. As a result of all of this, therapy is less about eradicating the depression, and more about listening carefully to it and learning how to navigate our way through it. A low mood can help to align our behavior with our values, but too much of it can result in a state of shutdown.

**

Respite – Signs that your depression has tipped you into a state of shutdown

How to recognize the signs of depression:

- A persistently low mood
- Frequently negative thoughts
- A lack of energy
- Heavy limbs
- A feeling of detachment from people or objects
- Tearfulness and sadness
- Oversleeping, problems sleeping, or problems going back to sleep
- Overeating or undereating
- Overworking
- Difficulty concentrating on tasks
- Anger and irritability

**

I can often spot depression in the self-statements that people use. Often problems are created by our *reaction* to an event more than the event itself, and that reaction is manifested in self-statements like "I am powerless," "I must not show I care about this," or "I always get everything wrong." Someone might be trapped in a relationship where they believe that they should not feel certain things, let alone communicate those feelings. These trapped feelings, whether they are sadness, anger, despair, or even rage, can leave someone walking through their life feeling flattened or despondent. They have learned that their emotions are unacceptable, and so they have learned to shut them off for the sake of others. A big part of the work involves helping someone to expand their vocabulary in terms of emotion words, identifying the emotions that apply to them, and helping them to come to terms with their own feelings. This can also involve checking for blind spots because depression can make us adopt an unhealthily cyclopic focus on our deficits. An attempt to address this is not a case of toxic positivity, where you are dismissing someone's suffering. It is an attempt to address the imbalance that depression can cause, or, in other words, to address their *cognitive constriction* (when someone does not think clearly or comprehensively). As Kenneth France, professor of psychology at Shippensburg University, points out in his book *Crisis Intervention*, depressed and suicidal people can display signs of "cognitive restriction" which means a person's thinking has become so rigid that they are unable to identify solutions to their problems. As a result, when we are depressed, we sometimes need help to find our way out of this Internal Prison. Although this can involve being helped to see a wider perspective of our reality than our own myopic perspective, it is not a dismissal of our emotions. No matter how hopeless or dark our thoughts may become, our feelings are valid. To go beyond the confines of your Internal Prison of depression does not mean to stray from your core, but to strengthen it.

Beyond the confines of your low self-esteem

Mark Twain once wrote that "the worst loneliness is to not be comfortable with yourself." What is the point of an open prison door when your self-esteem keeps you trapped? Self-esteem means a sense of worth, no matter what you achieve or own, no matter the external gains you have enjoyed. Self-esteem is an *internal* sense of value, and it is a concept that is assessed over a long period of time. It is not a flash-in-the-pan moment of satisfaction. Your self-esteem isn't just based on your current life, and no matter how many years pass, those early moments with your caregivers can leave a wounded sense of self-esteem that takes time to heal. Even if your caregivers did not intend this, you may have been left with an unequivocal message that *you don't matter*. I am painfully conscious not to fall into this trap with my own children, especially when I end up working late on client issues or my latest book. The last thing I want to do is repeat the experiences I had during my own childhood, when there were clear messages communicated, whether intentionally or not, that I did not matter. This leaves a wound on a person's self-esteem, but it is not a severance of your spirit. It can heal with the help of healthy, balanced relationships in your current life.

You can't see oxygen, but you can recognize the deprivation of it in the blueness of someone's pallor, and similarly you cannot see self-esteem, but it is easy to recognize the lack of it in someone's behavior. They might appear overly anxious to please others, or they might act with aggression, or they might turn to substances or alcohol with more frequency, or they might overdo it when it comes to exercise, eating, working, or even posts on social media. Even someone who appears confident, who endlessly attends social gatherings, might lack self-esteem when you realize that they only ever stay for a short time, and they never engage in conversation beyond a quick exchange of pleasantries. Deep down, they lack the self-esteem to believe that anything about them is worthy of attention, but they are trying to mask this lack of self-esteem with an abundance of activity. Charging through this person's veins is a sense of shame. It will take a bit of unpacking to get to the source of this shame, but without doing so, this person will continue to feel empty and probably exhausted by all the superficiality.

Shame is like a black hole that emerges from within. It devours anything that you once held dear, and any semblance of value that you might have seen in yourself. If it is not stopped, it will consume the whole of you. Unlike guilt, which says something about what you have done (or not done), shame is about who you are. "Bad, inside and out" is how one person described it. Others use phrases like "I am dirty," "I am unlovable," or "I am unworthy." Too often in my practice I see shame being carried by people who were abused, and it can take a long time for people to hand that shame back to the perpetrator (metaphorically, of course). After all, the shame is rightfully the perpetrator's, not the survivor's, to carry. In her book *Narrative Approaches to Working with Adult Male Survivors*, Kim Etherington points out how difficult it can be when the perpetrator was a caregiver. In this relationship the caregiver held the keys to your survival because you depended on them for survival (food and shelter, for example). If they abused their power, you had a stark choice: Accept their abuse by distorting yourself to accommodate that discomfort, or resist and run the risk of that food and shelter being withdrawn, which would ultimately mean that you would not survive. When you distort yourself to accommodate the discomfort of the abuse, you can get stuck in this process of adaptation, and even when you have grown up and moved far away from that abusive caregiver, you can remain stuck in a tendency to ignore your inner cues. For example, you can learn to shut down your awareness during playful or pleasurable moments, so you are numb, because this is what you once did as a child to survive. As we saw earlier in this book, this method of shutdown, in the form of numbing or memory loss, for example, is called dissociation. It takes a great deal of work with a trained professional to learn new ways, and to respond to your internal cues of discomfort or pleasure rather than shutting them off. It also takes a great deal of hard work to learn that not all relationships are comprised of an abusive imbalance of power. Trust, even intimacy, is possible, with the right person.

Self-esteem can be torn down by an incessantly negative inner critic. When this occurs, it is important to distinguish between constructive self-feedback and a tendency to self-bully. A key part of this distinction is to ask yourself: *What is within my control to change?* Whatever is within your control to change can be the subject of healthy, constructive self-feedback. However, constantly criticizing yourself for things that are outside of your control is likely to be self-bullying. We all have hopes and dreams, but when these turn into unrealistic expectations that we constantly set for ourselves, we can turn our lives into a perpetual misery. Another healthy distinction is between taking responsibility and constantly blaming yourself. Taking responsibility often involves a less absolute view of things, where more than just your part in a situation is taken into account. I often tell my clients that they can avoid absolute self-blame by acknowledging *all* the factors involved with whatever went wrong. Self-blame often oversimplifies events, focusing too much on your own part in all of it. Under such an intense spotlight, is it any wonder we retreat to the cool confines of our Internal Prison?

The gift of presence

Low self-esteem often shows itself in a sense of restlessness. We are uncomfortable in our own skin and so we constantly race from one distraction to another. Maybe there is a fear that if we stop for a moment and let reality catch up with us, it will all feel pointless. Who wouldn't want to run from such a feeling? You know the adage about running from your problems and how eventually they will catch up with us? We need to stop running from our own self-image and really look at who we are. We cannot change things that are outside of our awareness, and so if things do not feel right but we are unsure why (one of the hallmarks of depression), we need to slow down and stop trying to distract ourselves from ourselves. Only when we gain awareness and accept all that we are can we truly change and grow. This mindful awareness of who we are, right now, can help us to grow from within, gaining a sense of comfort in our own skin. This usually leads us to outgrow the Internal Prisons we once created, like an orchid outgrows a pot in which it was once confined.

For many years, Abigail tried to ignore her trembling hands and legs, always hoping that the deadweight of gloom that dragged at her heart would somehow leave her all on its own.

She kept telling herself that she was too busy to talk to anyone about this, and her own mother had been medicated up to the eyeballs, so she didn't want to slip into the same blank-eyed stare. She resented those long dark childhood days when her mother retreated from the world. She thought about all the opportunities she missed out on, the playdates and sporting activities she could have been taken to if her mother weren't so lost to her own depression. The depression was a dark weight that crushed any joy out of her mother's marriage to Abigail's father, who left when Abigail was nine years old. "Left me to her," Abigail would tell her husband, fighting back the tears if she was careless enough to let slip into her mind the image of that lonely nine-year-old. After her father left, Abigail and her mother struggled financially, and years later, Abigail's husband winced when he heard stories of her going hungry, or when the refrigerator broke down and they couldn't afford to replace it. They would hang the food in plastic bags out of the window of their third-floor apartment, and according to Abigail, the raccoons and squirrels usually got to it before they could eat it all.

Despite the discomfort of having to witness these stories, Abigail's husband was pleased that she had the courage to share her childhood with him because it explained why she would freak out at the sign of any wastage, and why she worked so hard, even though she had more than established herself in a top accounting firm. And it explained why she refused to take any time away from work to speak to a therapist about the things she had shared, things that sounded like depression, anxiety, or both.

She might have continued to try and ignore it, well aware that she was risking burnout, but when her daughter was born, she started to understand that there was another way beyond the rush to distract herself from her own self-image. All at once she realized that she could not continue to avoid those uncomfortable feelings that kept begging for attention. Having a child is a powerful moment in our lives when we are suddenly, from the moment of birth, faced with a simple choice: Continue with this frantic pace of distracting ourselves from our feelings and fight against these newborn moments of stillness, or give in and stop, allowing it all to flood in. Luckily, Abigail chose the latter. She accepted the help of a therapist, and together they exposed her, slowly and gently, to all those feelings that she was rushing from. At times this was extremely painful, digging into memories of her childhood that she had, for the most part, kept at a safe distance from her awareness. But after the initial pain subsided, she was able to incorporate the pain of her childhood with a clearer sense of self-identity. One important part of this was separating the shortcomings of her parents from her own self-worth.

To rebuild her self-esteem—or, in other words, to help Abigail get to a place where she could feel comfortable in her own skin—she had to learn to sit with her thoughts, emotions, and bodily sensations. There is a plethora of mindfulness exercises to help with this, and the idea is that you are not ruminating on your past, nor anxiously fearing a future that you cannot yet identify. Instead, you really sit in the moment, fully aware, sometimes even painfully aware, of everything about yourself, and you learn, slowly, to accept yourself. With that, you learn to savor the gift of *presence.*

**

Respite – How to rebuild your self-esteem

Mindfulness is an exceptionally helpful tool to rebuild your self-esteem. When people struggle with self-esteem, their minds become hijacked with thoughts and emotions about how they should change. Mindfulness offers a useful antidote to this tendency. When you practice mindfulness, you simply notice what *is*, without trying to change things. This is a skill that is becoming less and less common in this modern age of incessant technological distractions.

Set out in Chapter 2 of this book is just one example of a mindfulness exercise. There are plenty more on my website at www.chriswarrendickins.com.

Ideally, you should set aside time each day to engage in at least one mindfulness exercise. But don't judge yourself if you don't manage every day. It takes time to establish a new routine.

In addition to mindfulness, remember these key points about self-esteem –

- Assess how much your thoughts are getting stuck on regrets from the past, or fears of the future, rather than acknowledging the present reality.
- Make a choice to let certain negative thoughts go. You do not have to grab hold of each one.
- Strive for self-compassion, including an attempt to understand rather than criticize yourself.
- Remind yourself of the difference between a balanced evaluation of all factors, including everyone involved, rather than a distorted emphasis of your own part in what happened.
- Center yourself with your own values, not the latest trend followed by others.

**

Beyond the confines of your imposter

In *I'm a Joke and So Are You: Reflections on Humour and Humanity*, comedian Robin Ince writes, "The secret of the social human is to tactfully conceal the fact that you're screaming on the inside," and I think that pretty much sums up Imposter Syndrome. It is all very well trying to reach beyond the confines of your Internal Prison, but what if the Imposter is blocking your every route to freedom? No matter how many naysayers tried to talk you out of it, you made a success of your business. You have people who report to you, and a decent income, and yet still you believe you should not be in this role. You are certain that any day, people are going to find you out as some kind of fraud, or someone is going to come knocking at the door and end every aspect of happiness that you have dared to enjoy. Imposter Syndrome does not just pose a threat to your working life. When you are plagued by the belief *I am not good enough* it can leak into your personal life, too. If you do not believe that the relationship you have is what you deserve, or if you believe that things are going to go wrong at any moment, you can start to second-guess everything, and this can cause a huge strain on your relationships. I know of someone who refused to get married, no matter how much he and his girlfriend wanted to, because he doubted his ability to provide for his loved one. The Imposter blocked his every move, leaving him petrified that everything could be taken away from him at any moment—and so why expose his girlfriend, whom he loved so much, to the risk of this catastrophe?

The term Imposter Syndrome was first coined by psychologists Suzanne Imes and Rose Clance. When we suffer from it, we dismiss our achievements or minimize the significance of any gains in our life. For example, you passed the exams through school and college—in fact, you didn't just pass them but did really well. But still, you're certain there was probably a marking error plaguing each assessment, or perhaps standards have been diluted over the years, so your achievements are not evidence of true, objectifiable intelligence. Yes, you got the job, but this was only because they couldn't find anyone else, or they made a mistake, or you were so vague in the interview that they overestimated your abilities and experience. You fell in love, yes, but they are only going to stay with you until a better person comes along. You bought the house, but it will probably be repossessed any day now, after you lose the job that you do not deserve. Imposter Syndrome is the feeling that eventually the mask will slip, and everyone will discover that we are not who we say we are, that we are an Imposter. Imposter Syndrome can plague any walk of life, so the doctor believes that she will be found out as misdiagnosing her patients, and the financial adviser will be proven to have misguided people on their investments, and the college professor will be humiliated when all the students stand up and point at him, proclaiming him to be a fraud who has no right to teach. Imposter Syndrome can seriously undermine a person's ability to function, and it can lead to depression or anxiety.

The trouble is, when we believe the Imposter and work harder and harder, overpreparing for meetings or projects or clients, we can end up making the Imposter bigger and stronger, because we then believe that we only have our role because of the excessive work we put in. We also run the risk of creating a self-fulfilling prophecy because our excessive work can lead to burnout, manifesting itself in sleeplessness and poor concentration, for example, putting us at risk of really losing the job that we fear we never deserved in the first place.

Your self-talk has a big impact on how big and strong (and even ugly) this Imposter can be. The more punitive and judgmental our self-talk, the more likely our Imposter is going to overshadow any confidence we may have discovered. You can combat this by searching for a calmer, more compassionate voice, the type of voice you might reserve for loved ones such as your partner, child, or elderly parent. I know many people who say or write to themselves encouraging one-liners when they are feeling particularly tired, when they know that the Imposter is gaining ground on them simply because they have less energy to fight or flee it. This was particularly apparent during the COVID-19 pandemic, when people who had lived perfectly happily for years, with apparent confidence, lost their momentum and started to doubt their every move. One parent told me that she was "done, spent, without any fight left" after trying for months to keep a happy home while working from home and teaching her two young children. When we looked at this a little more, she realized that her self-talk had grown harsh and bitter. She was bitter that she could not go anywhere, and she was bitter that the schools were closed, and she was bitter that she did not know when the pandemic was going to end and whether her children would ever enjoy an education in a safe way again. Life had become one thankless task after another, and it was only when she stopped performing those tasks for just a moment that she realized how grueling life had become. But it didn't have to continue that way. With the help of a supportive friend, she started to give herself permission to take a day off from work now and then, and she set up little rewards for herself at the end of the working week. It was a very simple process, but the results were transforming.

Plenty of therapeutic approaches support this process, including the concept of *improving the moment* as developed by Marsha M. Linehan, a psychologist who created dialectical behavior therapy (DBT). Linehan used the anacronym IMPROVE to stand for Imagery (for example, "imagine being somewhere else or in a different situation"), Meaning (for example, "find some kind of meaning in the present moment"), Prayer, Relaxation, One thing in the moment (for example, "focus your entire mind on one thing in the moment"), Vacation (for example, "take a short vacation from the moment by briefly avoiding the situation"), and Encourage yourself.

Sometimes people experience what is called a *secondary gain* from their Imposter Syndrome. When someone has been brought up to believe that their identity is defined by the label others (usually their family) gives them, it can be hard to challenge this label. You might have experienced this yourself, where your parents always referred to you as the "sensitive one," or the "bookish one," or the "outgoing life and soul of the party."

Take Mary, for example, who was always referred to as the "sporty one." When she discovered she was gifted in intelligence, she started to pursue a career as a neuroscientist. No matter how many years into this career she got, still she was referred to as the "sporty one." Mary would even hear her mother referring to her daughter as someone who has "boundless energy, so much that she cannot sit still long enough to read a sentence, let alone a book." Despite her consistently good performance in all exams, Mary began to doubt her academic ability. Imposter Syndrome had emerged in her life, and the secondary gain, or *payoff,* was a continuing relationship with a mother she loved. For Mary to be seen by her mother, she had to be the "sporty one," not the "academic."

When we are young, we are constantly evolving and learning endless amounts of information at the speed of light. We haven't the time or energy to stop and challenge the label we have been given. And when we are young, our brain is still developing, so even if we had the time or energy, we probably would not have the mental ability to do this. And then, when we get older, it can be even harder to act in a way that is inconsistent with that label. I have heard people condemn a family member as "crazy," or having some sort of "breakdown" simply because that family member decided, once and for all, to reject the label they never asked for in the first place. When family members refuse to relinquish the label, it is easy to see how the danger of depression increases. Suddenly a person has an impossible choice: lose a relationship with their family members or act in a way that is contrary to their true nature. This becomes even more complicated when that person is in a relationship. I have seen family members heap the blame onto this partner, as if they somehow "polluted" or "corrupted" their loved one. Again, the risk of depression increases when people are faced with the impossible choice of taking the side of a partner or family member.

No matter how many years elapsed, Mary still doubted her ability as a neuroscientist. The Imposter had a permanent place at her table because Mary believed that it gave her the secondary gain of a continuing relationship with her mother.

It is my hope that one day she will renegotiate that relationship without the need for an Imposter.

**

Respite – Imprisoning thought patterns on which the Imposter thrives

- Labeling: You call yourself "stupid" or "a failure."
- Filtering: You only focus on the negative.
- Polarized Thinking: (or Black-and-White Thinking): Things are an absolute disaster or an absolute success.
- Overgeneralization: You decide that one mistake will mean that you will not get anything right.
- Jumping to Conclusions: You assume people are thinking badly of you.
- Personalization: You focus only on your role in an incident, ultimately leading to self-blame.

**

It is painful enough when the Imposter leans on your own shoulder, but when you see him roughing up the self-esteem of your kids, then the fight is truly on. Imagine seeing your kids develop into kind, enthusiastic, and hardworking people, only to hear them in tearful moments dismiss any achievements as "pure luck" or things they don't really deserve. I have seen and heard children call themselves "stupid," or "not a born athlete," or "a no-hoper," and nothing is more painful to witness. Depending on their age, some children might benefit from a little guidance about the different types of imprisoning thought patterns that we are all prone to use. We tyrannize ourselves with the endless *shoulds* of unrealistic expectations, we use emotional reasoning to believe that just because we *feel* a certain way, that it is true. We personalize situations, placing all the blame on our shoulders, and we oversimplify life, creating a black-or-white reality. Our performance, for example, was *all* good or *all* bad. We read other people's minds, assuming they hate us or think we are incompetent, and we make assumptions that other people are enjoying their career and making boundless advances to early retirement or zillionaire status. We catastrophize, we generalize, and we adopt such a singularity in our approach that we cannot see the forest for the trees. And instead of appreciating some of our achievements, we discount those positives as worthless or mere flukes. All of this gives the Imposter plenty of material to use in their stand-up show that pokes holes in your confidence with every punch line. The more we can set ourselves free of these imprisoning thought patterns, the freer we are of the Imposter. This is an ongoing lesson that we can learn for ourselves so we can use it to help our children.

Since the pandemic, our ability to parent from within confines has been tested to the limit. And the challenges continue. We may have emerged from parenting within the confines of public health restrictions, but there is no normal to return to. And many communities were already struggling before the pandemic.

What do you need to parent from within the confines of such a changed world?

CHAPTER 5

Parenting within your confines

Tell me and I forget, teach me and I may remember, involve me and I learn.
- Benjamin Franklin

I can tell them to do things over and over again, and still they just point-blank refuse. I am really running out of patience, and it is destroying my relationship with these kids. There are times when I have screamed at them to keep going with their math homework or writing assignments, and it feels like I leave my body in those moments. I can see myself doing it, and I want to stop screaming, but something grips me from inside. I know how ridiculous it sounds. I am the parent, and they are just children. But knowing it doesn't help.

Maya was in tears when she said this. When the pandemic closed the schools and daycare facilities, Maya and her wife, Valerie, were met with the impossible task of homeschooling their children while they each held down a full-time career. Add in the uncertainty about getting sick, finding groceries, and trying to remain calm while they lived, worked, and educated under one roof, and it is no surprise that there was a distinct lack of logic from the rational prefrontal cortex. They were left under the rule of their inelegant limbic system, and their amygdalae were sounding the alarm of *danger*, keeping them in an exhaustingly heightened state of alert. According to Polyvagal Theory, they were in the fight-or-flight survival mode of the sympathetic nervous system, so there was no hope for calm and connected parenting using the *social engagement system* of the ventral vagal pathway.

We are all still recovering from those days of confinement, and even though the restrictions have been lifted, parents of school-aged children continue to have a heightened sense of concern about the emotional well-being of their children. And is it any wonder that we remain concerned? We have emerged from the confines of a pandemic to find a world that has changed beyond recognition. According to one report, many parents still say they are having "difficulties balancing their child's education and their work, household finances, and mental or physical health." Six in ten parents say the pandemic has negatively affected their children's schooling, and over half say the same about their children's mental health. In addition, half of adults overall say their own personal mental health has been negatively affected, and four in ten say the same about their physical health and their financial situation.

Doing it for the kids

UNICEF regularly carries out research into the well-being of children in what the organization calls "rich countries." According to its latest report card (published in September 2020), 'in twelve of forty-one countries, less than 75 percent of children aged fifteen have "high life satisfaction," and countries such as the United States, Malta, Republic of Korea, the United Kingdom, Japan, and Turkey scored the lowest. In addition, "suicide is one of the most common causes of death for adolescents aged 15 to 19." The jury is still out about the causes for these worrying statistics. Some say that the cause is less important than the solution, and the next report is due out shortly, so we will see whether there has been any improvement. Either way, we owe our children more. As a nation that is considered *developed*, the United States has plenty of resources to improve the life satisfaction of their young. And as this is a capitalist economy, perhaps investing resources might seem more appealing if we point to the high return on investment when we help people at a young age. Fewer adverse childhood experiences means less toxic stress to accumulate during the early years (while the brain is still developing), and a lesser likelihood for long-term damage to a person's mental and physical health. And a healthier nation overall is one that is better able to generate more productivity.

At the start of the pandemic, when Maya first told her wife that the schools were closing, they both laughed. "It will be cozy," Maya said with a smile, "all of us together under one roof for a few weeks. I am going to start baking again, in case the food supplies dwindle."

Little did they know that the school would remain closed for months, and how quickly their enthusiasm and hope faded. Just three months later Maya was screaming "This is a disaster!" when she discovered that the online lessons had been cancelled yet again, and for no apparent reason. "It's just one day" Valerie told her wife, attempting to reassure her while knowing that was a futile exercise. "The boys won't mind." Maya shook her head as she slammed the laptop shut. "*Just one day* today, on top of the *just one day* last week, and the countless other days during the previous weeks. This is their life, and they need to *learn!* They can't be left with a gaping hole in their education, and then be expected to survive this shitty world. What if this means they don't get a job, and then they can't support themselves, and . . ." Maya started to cry. Valerie wanted to support her, but she struggled to understand why Maya had unraveled so quickly. To Valerie, this was just a minor bump in the road at an early stage in their sons' education.

What Valerie did not appreciate was that education meant much more to Maya than just good grades. After being beaten by her mother's boyfriend, Maya had been kicked out of her home at seventeen, after her mother found out that she was queer. She did her best to support herself, sleeping on a series of friends' sofas and growing hungry. She still remembers those pangs of hunger today, but they were not as painful as the aching humiliation of knowing when she overstayed her welcome. She would catch it in sideways glances exchanged between her friends and their parents, a mixture of impatience and irritation. Maya was determined that she would never feel that lost again, so she clung to education like it was her shield against vulnerability. And this worked for a long time—until the pandemic hit.

Maya was lost in her own story. Her past felt so real that it blinded her to the pain she was inflicting in the present, the pain of fear when she screamed at her children. Education is important, but during a global pandemic there was bound to be a loss of momentum, a loss that could be made up. It is not so easy, however, to rectify the damage inflicted by adverse childhood experiences.

What happened in our childhood stays in our childhood. . .?

Why do you need to know about all that? The past is the past, right? That was years ago. They are too old and frail to hurt me now, or *They are long dead.*

In my psychotherapy practice, this is the sort of pushback I encounter when I inquire about a client's childhood.

I am the parent now, and they are the children. I need to focus on the present, on the actual children who are running around in front of me, screaming and shouting and waking the neighbors. I have to keep them out of danger, out of trouble, away from the wrong crowds, and keep their minds on their schoolwork. I haven't the time to look back twenty or thirty years, to wonder what might have happened, what I felt then or feel now. The past is the past, right?

The trouble is that unhealed trauma often does hurt your ability to parent as much as it does your career, your intimate relationships, and your ability to concentrate on things you want to enjoy. Golfing, gaming, hanging out with your friends—these can all be impacted by childhood trauma. And if you are not careful, you can continue the cycle and create adverse experiences for your own children.

There is method in madness, and there are reasons why we act in certain ways. You don't just decide to see red or lash out, verbally or physically. You don't just decide to become easily startled and jumpy, restless like your nerves are on fire. You don't suddenly think how funny it would be to throw a stapler through the window or smash a chair into the wall. It just happens, in the blink of an eye, making you as confused as the people who witness it. Suddenly withdrawing from people, including the people you love, is equally beyond your immediate control. You don't just decide to detach and feel numb, cold, like a wasteland where emotion once lived. You are as unsure why you suddenly have a blank-mind, or gaps in your memory, as you are when you see red. But the method in what feels like madness is that maybe, just maybe, this is evidence of adverse experiences from your own childhood. In other words, all of this could be symptoms of trauma. We have seen how trauma can manifest itself in feeling too much *or* too little. When you feel too much, your whole body might feel like it is on fire, or you become drenched in sweat. Or your mind races and you are jumpy, on edge, certain something catastrophic is just about to happen. When you feel too little, there are gaps in your memory, or you feel checked out, not really in your body, let alone in the room. There is a disconnect between mind and body.

Psychiatrist Judith Herman explains the *dialectic of trauma* in her book *Trauma and Recovery*. That is, when we feel too much, we experience hyperarousal. When we feel too little, we experience hypoarousal. When we are in either one of those states, we are outside of our *window of tolerance*. As a result, we are not able to function as effectively as we would like, or connect calmly and compassionately with others, especially our children. It is exhausting enough to be stuck on a seesaw of hyperarousal and hypoarousal, but when you add the exhaustion of parenthood, and the pandemic (with all the fallout from it in the last two years), it is easy to see how some families are at breaking point. Trauma elevates your baseline, and so the near miss on the highway, the spilled juice box, and the playful shrieks from your children can shoot your nerves off the charts and outside your window of tolerance. You simply do not have the bandwidth.

Childhood abuse is not just delivered with violence and aggression. It can be hard to detect the absence of something, and for client and therapist, the absence of emotional warmth, support, and validation can slip through the cracks of detection or sit staring at you in the mirror, like a smile without the telltale lines around the eyes.

As we saw earlier in this book, adverse childhood experiences can include humiliation at the hands of your caregivers, your caregivers swearing at you or making you afraid you might be hurt, your caregivers' failure to meet your physical needs (such as clothing, food, or shelter), or growing up in a family where you do not feel special. Adverse childhood experiences also include sexual abuse (from an adult or from another child who was at least five years older than you), your caregivers separating or divorcing, witnessing domestic violence, and someone in your household struggling with mental health issues, drink, drugs, or going to prison.

Maya eventually told Valerie about the beating from her mother's boyfriend, but she said that her mother's silent treatment hurt so much more. Before she was kicked out of her home, her mother would spend days refusing to talk to her. Maya never understood what she had done to cause this, but her mother would wither her with a glance, scanning her daughter from head to toe, and dismissing her with a look of absolute disgust. It felt like Maya's whole appearance, and manner, her whole being, was being slowly picked apart by her mother, as if she were teasing the threads of a freshly stitched wound. As a result, Maya never believed she had any worth—and why would she when her own mother never acknowledged it? As Bessel A. van der Kolk wrote in *The*

Body Keeps the Score: "If your parents' faces never lit up when they looked at you, it's hard to know what it feels like to be loved and cherished. If you come from an incomprehensible world filled with secrecy and fear, it's almost impossible to find the words to express what you have endured. If you grew up unwanted and ignored, it is a major challenge to develop a visceral sense of agency and self-worth." Motivation and a desire or will to nurture ourselves, and therefore to nurture our children, can only come from this visceral sense of agency and self-worth. If this worth was never recognized by our own caregivers in the first place, it can be difficult to create from scratch.

Difficult, but not impossible.

So you want to just blame it all on the parents, some people say. Despite all the neuroscience to support concepts such as childhood trauma, the amygdala and limbic system, and the sympathetic and parasympathetic nervous systems, when we flick through the pages of people's childhood, it can seem to some that we are trying to find the Wolf to their Red Riding Hood, or the Wicked Stepmother to their Cinderella. But telling your trauma story is not about faultfinding. Parenting is one of the hardest experiences there is, and often parents are trying their best with what they have. You really wanted to return home calmly and ask each child, with composure, how their day was. And you really intended to listen to each answer and point out one or two insightful things that they could take away and learn from, small seeds of hope or resilience or love that they can hold and propagate over the years, giving them nourishment and comfort in your lifetime and beyond. You did not want to trip on the school bag they left by the front door any more than you wanted to stub your toe and spill your dinner on the carpet that had just been cleaned after the last disaster. You wish they could stop speaking at the same time, or stop hurting each other, or stop losing their homework when it feels like everyone else's children remember what they would have to do, how, and by when.

However, all these mismatches in hopes and expectations, and the messy, painful, loud, and annoying reality, cannot be used to deny the impact adverse childhood experiences have on a person's current life. The greater number of adverse childhood experiences during the first eighteen years of your life, the greater the impact on your health for the rest of your life. These experiences may trap us in a fight-or-flight response, where our sympathetic nervous system is overly active, producing toxic stress through an overproduction of hormones such as cortisol and adrenaline. Studies show that toxic stress can lead to increased blood pressure, heart disease, and diabetes, to name a few physical conditions.

When the jailer is your wounded inner child

For some, it can be helpful to conceptualize the impact of childhood trauma as the creation of a wounded inner child. As a result of these early experiences, you can, in your adulthood, become confined by your traumatized inner child. No matter how many times you try to escape it, no matter how many years you are into being a full-fledged adult who is responsible for other children, that inner child can take control. The wounds of your inner child might be ruptured by the trigger of a sudden association with the past trauma, which can be as innocuous as the sudden jolt of a slammed door, the thud of approaching footsteps, or the piercing stab of your own child's shriek. No matter how much you love your children, no matter how many times you tell yourself to keep your cool, something switches in you, and you lose it. Or you shut down. Or you break down—and all just because you stepped on a light saber sticking up from the hands of a miniature Luke Skywalker on the floor. You are trapped in this cycle as if your wounded inner child is your own internal jailor. You can see beyond the prison bars how other parents seem to laugh off these minor moments of irritation or surprise. You can see how calmly other parents kneel to their child's eye level, to gently explain why it is not cool to keep whacking someone over the head with their hard plastic toys. And you can see how much other parents seem able to fluidly interact with their children, other people's children, and other parents, while holding down a full-time job and tending to their intimate relationship, all during a pandemic or its fallout.

Still the inner wounded child is not bothered by what other people might be doing outside this prison. They just want to keep you safe so you (they) never experience that trauma again. They think that you are still a child, and when a child is in charge of other children, the likelihood of chaos breaking out seems pretty high—just as likely as you are to lose your cool and cause emotional disturbance for your own children. This is how a vicious cycle is created, if we are not careful.

But the cycle can be broken. If we can convince our wounded inner child that they are safe now, and that we now, as adults, have more strength and resources than that vulnerable child of the past once did, we can switch from a fight-or-flight response of our sympathetic nervous system, or a shutdown response of our dorsal vagal pathway, to an engaged, connected, and healing approach using the *social engagement system* of our ventral vagal pathway.

Regulating and co-regulating our way through parenting

When we are in the ventral vagal state, we can parent our inner child and the actual children we have as an adult. Sometimes it takes a therapeutic relationship to establish this sense of safety, and sometimes we can establish it with family or friends. No matter how we establish it, this safety is essential so we can learn to fluidly move up and down the ladder of our autonomic nervous system as the context requires, from connection into a protective stance and back to connection again. When we start to feel safe, we can enjoy the reciprocity that defines connectedness. When we feel safe enough to engage our *social engagement system*, we soften our tone, we slow our heart rate, and we appear calmer. In this ventral vagal state, our own autonomic nervous system communicates with the autonomic nervous system of our actual children, bringing a sense of attunement and resonance.

Imprisoning messages from your past

When we grow up with messages from our caregivers, communicated explicitly and implicitly, that we have no value or are unlovable, we can develop imprisoning beliefs that distort our approach to parenting.

When her mother forced Maya to leave her family home at seventeen, after finding out about her sexuality, she punctuated a series of messages that had been communicated very clearly throughout her childhood. Maya was unlovable, Maya was not a priority, and Maya would never be good enough. Research shows that adverse childhood experiences have a significant impact on our ability to love or trust each other, let alone love or trust ourselves. No matter how hard Maya tried at school, she was constantly criticized. She was too loud or putting on weight or not outgoing enough with her friends. If Maya showed any emotion, she was quickly dismissed as *ridiculous, melodramatic*, or *foolish,* so she learned to stay silent, sometimes finding release from these confusing emotions by cutting her inner thighs. All of these experiences, and the messages that were punctuated by them, still hurt Maya more than the pangs of hunger during those years of homelessness. She had no sure footing to pivot and twist from when, years later, she had to face the constant curveballs that parenting throws.

Our own adverse childhood experiences can confine our parenting as if we are stuck inside a bottle carrying these unhelpful messages. We can repeat some of the mistakes that our parents might not have made if they had benefited from the research that is now available about adverse childhood experiences (and the impact on our physical and mental health). When Maya loses her temper and screams at her children about their schoolwork, she is at risk of continuing the cycle by communicating to her own children—consciously or not, explicitly or implicitly—that they are never good enough, or that they are unlovable. We tend to do what we know, and what we know often comes from what has been taught to us by others, even when we also know it is wrong. Often this is a matter of lacking options. We would do it differently if we could just envision what that looks like, but when we have lacked supportive and compassionate caregivers as role models, reinventing our preconceived notion of parenting seems impossible or unnatural.

One afternoon I watched a cardinal as it hopped along the lawn with three of its young following closely behind. Each time the parent cardinal would stoop to tap the ground and then glance around, seemingly searching for sustenance, the young would mimic their elder. There was no hesitation, and it is easy to see how young birds take that first heart-stopping leap from the nest. It is natural that we learn from our elders. But when it comes to parenting our own children, it is never too late to learn something new.

**

Respite – Imprisoning messages from your past

Answer some of these questions, and then discuss your answers with your partner and decide whether each is something you view as important when parenting your own children:

- What expectations did your parents have of you during an average day?
- How did your parents want you to behave around them?
- What did your parents do when you disobeyed them?
- How were you punished?
- How were you rewarded?
- What happened when your views conflicted with their views?

- Were you aware of their emotions?
- Were you aware of your own emotions?
- For the first eighteen years of your life:
  - What was the worst moment?
  - What was the best moment?

**

How to parent your inner child and the children you care for

What is good for the goose is good for the gander. What we might need to learn about parenting our actual children can also apply to parenting our wounded inner child. Your inner child might have felt scared at times, particularly when you were physically smaller, or vulnerable, or hurt. If a situation in the present makes you feel like moments from your past—or in other words, if you are *triggered*—you can end up acting or speaking from that inner child. For example, you might lash out because you feel smaller than you really are. Or you might leave the house because you feel trapped, believing you have no other options. We are more likely to get triggered when we are parenting young children because there are frequent situations that can leave us stressed or exhausted, with or without a pandemic, and so we can end up feeling as vulnerable or overwhelmed as we once did as a child.

How would you respond to your own child if they showed that they were scared or hurt? Might you stop what you are doing and acknowledge the fear or pain that they are communicating? You wouldn't tell them that they did not feel that way, or they should not feel that way. You would respond in a way that validates their emotions, and you would show them—because you are the bigger, more experienced adult—that you are here to support and contain their fears or pain. Sometimes this can be healing in itself. We can parent by listening to and comforting our wounded inner child as much as we need to listen to and comfort our actual children. Doing this can create a sense of safety, and we know from Polyvagal Theory that when we *neurocept* (sense) safety, we are more likely to move up the ladder of our autonomic nervous system out of the shutdown of the dorsal vagal pathway, or the fight-or-flight of our sympathetic nervous system, and into the *social engagement system* of our ventral vagal system. If we can do this, we can regulate ourselves and co-regulate by connecting with others, particularly our children. If we can get to a ventral vagal state, we are less likely to lash out at imagined demons that hide in the shadows of our memories and haunt our wounded inner child.

Emotion regulation – The steady parent

Peter was a thirty-six-year-old airline pilot and parent to three school-aged children. Since the pandemic, Peter's wife, Denise, had seen a change in her husband. He was starting to take his frustrations out on the children, and on a handful of occasions she had witnessed him manhandling them during the weekend morning rush to sporting activities. The youngest tried to laugh it off, but you could see that the older two were shaken. Denise knew that Peter had a short fuse, and he was strangely jumpy even when she tried to joke with him. He could not stand being surprised by a hug or kiss from behind—but she never expected him to take it out on the children.

Peter knew that he should seek help but he genuinely didn't know where to begin. As the local ice hockey champion and naturally very tall, Peter was viewed by people outside of the family as the big, strong, dependable one—the hero in a way—and so the thought that he might need help was beyond comprehension for most people in his life. It was also beyond his own comprehension. Talking to someone about feelings was for women—a view that is held by many people, not just men. I discuss this at length in *Beyond the Blue*, but in brief, society is set up to expect the male labeled to remain strong, silent, and independent. As a result, we don't want to see or hear about their emotions or vulnerabilities. Peter is the big, strong ice hockey champion. If he doesn't have a grip on things, who does? Eventually his wife told him that if he did not get some sort of help with anger management, she would leave him. Peter's own parents had divorced when he was seven years old, so this was the last thing he wanted for his own children.

When Peter started therapy, he was desperate to find a way forward with his children. I find that some people will only seek therapy if they are at a crisis point, in part because of a misguided perception that therapy only fixes what is broken. I prefer to view it as part of a multifaceted approach to ensuring a healthy, balanced life—like a Swiss Army penknife with its many different components. One of the first tasks of therapy is to help the person identify and regulate their emotions. Before you can regulate your emotions, you need to identify them, understand their purpose, and learn how to use them to your advantage. Unregulated emotions can hijack you, and when you are a parent, your whole family becomes hostages. Emotion regulation can involve turning the volume up, if you are feeling particularly disconnected, for example, or turning the volume down, if things have become too much. I find that many of my clients never had the chance to learn about emotion regulation, either because of an invalidating and unsupportive childhood, or because their schooling and work life were focused on achievement and rational knowledge at the expense of emotional knowledge.

The damage of invalidation

To regulate our emotions, we need to acknowledge them without trying to deny or distort them. If we can learn to do this for our own emotions, we can do it for the emotions our children are trying to communicate. Denise was particularly concerned about Peter's attitude towards his sons, whom he was always telling to *toughen up*. Denise spoke of several occasions when their boys had shown sadness over being left out of a friend's birthday gathering, disappointment when they did not pass the wrestling tryout, or fear of an intimidating student in their class. "*So what?*" Peter would say. "I don't have time for emotions. I need my boys to make a success of their life, so they need to keep it moving and focus on other things. If we all sit around in sadness or disappointment, how will we get anything done?" I can understand Peter's fears, and he just wants the best for his children. But when we deny or distort emotions, our own or our children's, we can create an invalidating environment.

And the trouble with emotions is that the less aware we are of them, or the more we deny or distort them, the stronger they become. They tend to get louder . . . and louder . . . and louder, until we cannot ignore them any longer. As Marsha M. Linehan, psychologist and creator of dialectical behavior therapy (DBT), explains in the *DBT Skills Training Manual*, invalidating your child's emotions sends a message that the emotions are not heard. What happens when you are in a crowded restaurant, and you think the person sitting opposite to you does not hear everything? You repeat yourself, only this time a little louder. This is known as *escalation*, and it can take the form of many different types of behaviors. For example, after Peter's son was sad about the friend's birthday, and this sadness was invalidated, Peter's son started to kick the family's dog. In response, Peter became angry at his son for hurting the dog, escalating things further. Now Peter not only invalidated his son's sadness, but he also started punishing his son. Angry and resentful, Peter's son stormed off, but not before he threw a curse word over his shoulder, making his father explode, grab his son's arm, and slap his legs with his bare hand.

Invalidating environments tend to over- or underreact to a person's emotional needs, leading to that person's inability to learn how to regulate themselves. In contrast, a validating environment responds with seriousness and concern for a person's emotional needs, and the response is proportionate and appropriate. Once emotions are invalidated, the escalation can take many harmful forms including anger and aggression, withdrawal, substance abuse, self-harm, and suicidal ideation.

**

Respite – How to identify an invalidating environment

Just some of the words used in an invalidating environment -

- "Stop crying, you have no reason to cry."
- "You don't feel that way, you are lying."
- "Stop overreacting like that, you are being melodramatic."
- "Go away if you are going to cry, I don't want to see it."
- "Your tears are manipulative."
- "You are so stupid."
- "You are a bad child."
- "You are crazy."
- "You shouldn't feel like that because no one else does."

**

To remain a steady pilot during this parenting journey, you need to learn how to *identify different emotions* in order to regulate them. As we have mentioned earlier in this book, emotions usually consist of one word, so if you are using more than one word, you are probably describing a thought. The more comprehensive vocabulary you have to identify your emotions, the better chance you have of regulating those emotions. In other words, the more accurately the word reflects your emotion, the closer you can get to meeting the need that could be at the heart of that emotion. For example, you might feel angry or disgusted or sad or happy or surprised or bad or fearful. But within each of those broad emotions is a the finely tuned version of it.

Is it just anger, or is it frustration, feeling mad, bitterness, aggression, humiliation, feeling let down, distant, or critical?
Is it indignance, fury, jealousy, betrayal, resentment, disrespect, ridicule, annoyance, dismissive, infuriated, or numb, even?
You may be disgusted, but are you repelled, disapproving, disappointed, or do you feel awful?
Do you feel nauseated, embarrassed, appalled, revolted, judgmental, detestable, horrified, or hesitant?
You might feel sad, but do you actually feel despair, vulnerable, guilty, lonely, depressed, or hurt?
Or perhaps even empty, ashamed, powerless, grief, isolated, embarrassed, abandoned, fragile, remorseful, or disappointed?
If you feel happy, do you actually feel optimistic, content, interested, proud, or peaceful?
Or do you feel powerful, accepted, trusting, thankful, free, intimate, joyful, curious, inspired, inquisitive, successful, confident, loving, valued, hopeful, or courageous?
If you are surprised, do you feel startled, confused, excited, or amazed?
Or maybe disillusioned, energetic, eager, in awe, dismayed, shocked, astonished, or perplexed?
If you feel bad, are you stressed, bored, tired, or busy?
Or are you unfocused, out of control, overwhelmed, pressured, or apathetic?
If you feel fearful, do you feel scared, anxious, threatened, weak, rejected, or insecure?
Or are you nervous, overwhelmed, persecuted. worthless, helpless, excluded, insignificant, worried, or frightened?

You need to identify the one-word emotion that you feel, but you also need to identify it in others, including your children. You can do this by tracking a person's facial expressions, tone of voice, pace of speech, and other such signs. You also need to help your children recognize their own emotions and the emotions of others. In *Permission to Feel: Unlocking the Power of Emotions to Help Our Kids, Ourselves and Our Society Thrive*, Marc Brackett, founding director of the Yale Center for Emotional Intelligence and professor in the Child Study Center at Yale University, writes about studies that show that an ability to identify a wide range of emotions is "linked to lower activation of the amygdala" (our brain's alarm system) and "higher activation in the right ventrolateral prefrontal cortex (RVLPFC), which supports emotion regulation."

Emotion regulation also involves a recognition of *the degree of intensity of those emotions*. Some things feel more important than others, and to recognize this in ourselves and our children helps to guide our responses. We learn when things require us to drop everything and hold our child, and when they just need a smile or a quick hug. Some people find it helpful to rate the intensity of an emotion on a scale of 0 to 10, and I know children find this particularly useful.

When Peter started to acknowledge the sadness that his sons were communicating, this seemed to help, without the need to find any solutions. Just hearing their sadness, communicating that he could understand why they felt this way, and showing that it was okay to feel this way, was a powerful moment in his parenting. It was a useful first step, although he would have a long way to go after that.

**

Respite – Help with emotions

Some prompts to help your child with their emotions:

- "What's going on?"
- "We can talk if you want to. I am here when you need me."
- "Would you like to catch up on things together?"
- "How do you feel right now?"
- "Can you point to some pictures in that book or comic, to show me how you feel right now?"
- "For each feeling or emotion, how intense do you feel it, on a scale of 0 to 10 (where 10 is the most intense)?"
- "For each feeling or emotion, use some different colors to rate the intensity."
- "What was happening before you felt like that?"
- "What was happening while you felt like that?"
- "What was happening after you felt like that?"
- "What ideas do you have about why you feel that way?"
- "How do you want to feel instead?"
- "Would you like to brainstorm some ideas about how you might be able to feel that way instead?"
- "How might it look if things were how you want them to be? Can you describe that for me?"
- "Do you want to draw a picture to show me that?"

**

You can use your body to identify emotions, even those not immediately in our awareness. We can feel it in our gut, in our throat, in our chest, or even in our restless hands and feet. We need to assess whether these physical sensations are caused by something physiological (hunger, dehydration, or a physical health condition, for example), or whether it is our emotions.

This is not an easy process, and it is made harder when we rush from one distraction to the next. We are so preoccupied by our children, our partner, our work life, and the latest gems of wisdom on Twitter or TikTok, that we neglect a valuable source of information: our body. As we saw with an invalidating environment, if we ignore our bodies, whatever the body is attempting to communicate only gets louder. This could be an escalation in the level of pain or tightness in our body or, after being ignored for so long, our body can fall silent. We can become detached from it, or numbed, as if we are just dreaming our way through life on autopilot. Not a great way to spend the only days we have, this one life we have been given. The solution is simple, and yet because it is so simple, people dismiss it. You just need to carve out a handful of minutes each day to stop listening to all the information from external sources and ask yourself such open-ended questions as:

- "How am I feeling today?"
- "No really, how am I truly feeling today?"
- "Am I sure I have identified everything that is coming up for me right now?"
- "How does my body feel?"
- "Do any of my bodily sensations suggest any particular emotions? Why?"
- "Why might I be feeling this way?"
- "How helpful or unhelpful is this for me?"
- "What might I do about this?"
- "Can I think of three things that might help with that?"
- "What support do I need?"

The *so what* of your emotions, and the emotions of your children

Emotions are important sources of information. Our emotions might tell us that something needs to change, or that this is important to us, or that it is so important that it should take priority over everything else right now. Each emotion will communicate a particular type of information. For example, sadness alerts us to our losses or failed goals, and this might help another person understand that we need support in the form of a smile or a hug. Anger tells us that we may have had our rights violated, or that people should back away for now, and it helps us to defend our boundaries. Fear alerts us to escape danger, or that we are likely to lose something of value if we don't take evasive action. Happiness helps us to recognize things that we value while love helps us to attach to others.

There are no good or bad emotions, although there may be good or bad consequences to acting (or not acting) on those emotions. We need to balance our emotions with other sources of information, including our rational mind. Too much of a good thing is unwise, so if we act only according to our emotions, we end up a volatile mess of volcanic eruptions. Yet if we act only according to cool, hard logic, we come across as a robot. Combined with our rational mind, our emotions can help us to achieve a balanced approach, helping us respond in a healthy, proportionate way to whatever life puts before us. Before a presentation at work, we need an increase in adrenalin to focus our mind, and this elevated level of attention also makes us sound interested and interesting. But too much fear, to the point of assuming mortal danger, and we end up blank-minded and frozen. The same can be said for a lack of trust in others. We need to assess how much we should share with each person and whether we should believe what they say, but if we disbelieve everyone at every moment, we will end up isolated.

Once you accurately name the emotion, its intensity, and its purpose, you need to decide what to do about it. You may need to communicate that emotion, or there might be an adjustment you need to make in order to regulate it. Sometimes the intensity of an emotion can be unhelpful, so you may need to turn the volume up or down. This is essential because, as

Brackett explains, the excess stress hormone (cortisol) in our brain can inhibit the prefrontal cortex from functioning properly. We literally cannot think straight.

This is what both Peter and Maya had to learn about screaming at their kids. When they did this, they ended up achieving nothing because the brains of their kids went offline the moment they were scared of their parents. Using Polyvagal Theory to understand this, if Peter and Maya's children were screamed at to the point of fear, their autonomic nervous system would fall back down the ladder to either the fight-or-flight of the sympathetic nervous system, the dorsal ventral vagal state of shutdown, or the *servitude and ingratiation* of the fawn response. In either case, they were not in an optimum position to listen to their parent or learn from them.

It is ironic that Maya was screaming at her children because she wanted them to have a good education. The reality is that children are unable to learn effectively when they are not emotionally regulated. In fact, education is enhanced when we can integrate the use of emotions in the learning process. Brackett refers to the work of Mary Helen Immordino-Yang, professor of Education, Psychology and Neuroscience at the University of South Carolina. Immordino-Yang explains that "children learn what they care about," and "attention, focus, and memory," the most important parts of learning, "are all controlled by our emotions, not cognition . . . When students feel deeply engaged and connected in the learning process, and when what they learn is relevant and meaningful to their own lives, there is activation in the same brain systems (for instance, the medulla) that keep us alive."

If we are to learn about emotion regulation for our own emotions but also to help our children regulate theirs, we need to have at our disposal as many strategies as possible. What might work at one time in your life may not work well later on, and the same goes for your children. Luckily, there are as many different methods of emotion regulation as there are shades of color.

- *Mindfulness*, the practice of letting go, or "non-doing" as Kabat-Zinn calls it, can create a space between your emotions and your response. The more space you have, the easier it is to choose how to respond to your emotions, rather than to impulsively react.
- *Breathing exercises* are forms of emotion regulation. As mentioned earlier in this book, the vagus nerve runs through the lungs and heart, so breathing exercises can help you to change "the tone of the autonomic nervous system," writes Stephen W. Porges in *The Polyvagal Theory*. As Deb Dana explains in *The Polyvagal Theory in Therapy*, research shows that "slower breathing, prolonged exhalation, and resistance breathing" increase parasympathetic activity. This is our compassion nerve, so the more we can activate this, the easier it will be to regulate our emotions (and help our children do the same).
- *Visualizations* (for example, visualizing a safe or calm place, or visualizing a future state that you wish to achieve) are another form of emotion regulation.
- *Others* include social contact; physical exercise; reading or writing (including journaling); making art: eating a balanced diet; getting good sleep; challenging your assumptions and beliefs about yourself, others, and the world around you; distraction; and self-compassion.

When I talk to my clients about emotion regulation, it isn't the concept that is difficult for them, or even the variety of methods available. The problem is getting round to actually doing it. *I have so much going on at work* they say, or *We have just started a building project at home*, or *I keep forgetting because life gets in the way.* And I get it. I have fallen into this trap myself, when I have promised that things will be different, and yet, again, *life gets in the way.* Brackett suggests that we come up with an object (like a boundary) that symbolizes the start of the need to regulate your emotions around your children. For example, it could be the driveway to your house, or the car steering wheel that you grip as you drive home, or the keys you retrieve to open the door to your family home. Whatever the symbol, Brackett suggests that it is *that moment* when you make the conscious effort to regulate your emotions. It anchors the act in your brain, making it a part of your daily routine rather than a vague promise like *one day I will change the world.*

However, we also need to manage expectations. You aren't suddenly going to flip a switch and find that you are levitating on a cloud of tranquility because you can suddenly regulate your emotions. I can't tell you how many times clients have said to me *I tried it once*—whether it was mindfulness exercises, breathing exercises, journaling, or visualizations—*and it didn't work.* Brackett suggests that it takes about six months to develop the ability to regulate our emotions, and although I would caveat that everyone is different; this is a very rough indicator.

A prison of perfectionistic parenting

When you find out about the pregnancy, when you see the first heartbeat, when you see that misshapen blob on the sonogram that you are told is your baby, you know that you will do everything within your powers to love your child. You don't just know it—you *promise* them, and it is a deep promise of eternal commitment. And then you hold them for the first time, seeing how much they depend on you for their everything, and you promise them the same all over again. You will do everything you can to help them, to provide for them, and to help them navigate through life's vicissitudes.

It's quite a heady height to fall from when you realize that this is unsustainable. When your child pokes you in the eye for the fun of it (for the seventeenth time in a row), when they leave the car window open on the night of a storm, when the cat gets thrown across the room *just to see what happens*, and when they seem like they are just about to kill their siblings, you are bound to lose your patience. And then you cannot make it to their game, or you forget that they had an assignment due that night, and the fall from grace, the pop of the perfectionistic-parenting bubble, stings painfully. The reality is that you cannot and should not trap yourself within a prison of perfectionistic parenting.

Although they were not uncontroversial, Donald Winnicott and Bruno Bettelheim each helped parents give themselves permission to stop striving for perfectionism. In the 1970s, psychoanalyst and pediatrician Winnicott conceptualized the *good enough mother* in his famous book *Playing and Reality: The Child, the Family, and the Outside World.* In the 1980s, psychologist Bettelheim expanded this to the more inclusive *good enough parenting* in his book, *A Good Enough Parent.* In both cases, the emphasis was on a need for the child to experience frustrations now and again, so they learn to regulate their own emotions.

In the very early stages of development, an infant's dependence on their parents is appropriate, and it is expected that those parents sacrifice their own needs in favor of their newborn's. However, as the infant grows, the parents should gradually start allowing their child to experience frustration, starting slowly but eventually for longer periods of time. In other words, as parents we cannot, and should not, strive for perfection, attempting to eradicate all frustrations. Rather we should strive to be *good enough* parents. As Bettelheim explained, a parent should not "try to be a perfect parent, as much as one should not expect one's child to be, or to become, a perfect individual. Perfection is not within the grasp of ordinary human beings." In addition, perfectionism creates a blame culture where we become punitive instead of compassionate and understanding. When we as parents learn to accept our own imperfections, we find it easier to accept the imperfections in our children. This can be modeled to our children, so they learn to accept the imperfections in themselves and in other people.

When I am sad, I do not try and hide that from my children because it helps them to accept their own sadness. The same can be said for the loneliness, anger, and disappointment as much as the excitement, joy, and exhilaration of life. To be a good enough parent is to strike the right balance between parental love, comfort, and support, on the one hand, and self-awareness, self-soothing, and independence on the other. A good enough parent can also strike the balance between striving for the best and making the worst mistakes. No matter how many lessons we try to teach our children, it is with those scraps of freedom from imperfection that they learn how to fly.

Tik *Talk* Parenting

I can't get her off it. And worse, every conversation seems to revolve around something she has seen on that damn thing. And yet how much can she learn from it? These are mostly fifteen second videos of people lip-synching someone else's music. What is the point? People are so damn superficial these days that they haven't the attention span for a commercial, let alone a developed thought.

Patricia, a parent of a fourteen-year-old, was complaining about her daughter's poor performance at school. She hadn't yet been called for a meeting with the teacher or principal, but she knew this was going to be the next step after a series of poor grades. Patricia also noticed that her once-cheerful daughter was suddenly cynical and dismissive of things that used to bring her joy, particularly the friends she had hung out with. According to Patricia, the prime suspect to explain her daughter's recent transformation was TikTok.

Patricia's comments could have applied to any form of social media, but it was the new kid on the block that was the focus of her vitriol. Parents have understandably noticed the influence of this new form of online entertainment because in 2020 alone, TikTok increased its US user base by 85.3 per cent, a staggering increase to 65.9 million users. Some say that the pandemic helped to grow its popularity. While everyone was confined to their homes, TikTok offered a glimpse into the lives of other people—and hasn't this always been a form of entertainment? In the United Kingdom there was a program called *Through the Keyhole*, where we were taken on snooping safaris through the homes of famous people. And my American husband has told me about *Lifestyles of the Rich and Famous*. Isn't archeology a form of this, where we brush away sand and dirt to reveal the artwork and fine structures of the homes of our predecessors? So, the pleasures of TikTok have a long history.

We often blame the newcomer for our ills, and as we mentioned earlier in this book, little is known about the long-term impact of rapidly evolving technology. Pew Research reports that there are concerns that digital devices "give children easy access to inappropriate content and leave youth vulnerable to overuse and even bullying." In addition, "seven in ten parents think smartphones could bring more harm than good to children," and 54% of parents say "younger kids' engagement with these devices will hurt their ability to do well in school." Even more worrying, "six in ten parents say they are at least somewhat concerned about their child in this age range ever being the target of online predators (63%), accessing sexually explicit content (60%), and accessing violent content online (59%). Somewhat similar shares (56%) report they are very or somewhat concerned that their child might ever be bullied or harassed online."

Some argue that the growth in technology, or the inability to effectively monitor our children's use of that technology, is not as much of a concern as the structural inequality and privilege that exists in countries such as the US. This is a more pressing issue for our children, and one way it manifests itself is in the increasingly polarized views that divide us. It is all very well reaching beyond the confines of imprisoning messages from our past, short-circuited thought patterns, or emotion dysregulation, but if we are still confined by a lack of imagination (our own, or someone else's), and that takes the form of discrimination, intolerance, or outright aggression, still we are not free.

So, the question is: How can we reach beyond the confines of our imagination?

CHAPTER 6

Beyond the confines of our imagination

Men, even when they do not require one another's help, desire to live together.
- Aristotle

Let's face it: we go about our lives operating from an assumption that we are right. No matter how verifiable by science, years of research, or the black swan staring right at you, it can be hard to accept when we are wrong. We might have spent years believing in the existence of only white swans, and when our emotions get in the way, we find it hard to accept that our beliefs were misguided. And when we believe that we are right, we claim that we have evidence to show that others are wrong. Whether it is race, ethnicity, gender identity, sexuality, religion, neurodiversity, socio-economic groups, or disability, we label, blame, pathologize, and make an *other* of *them*, a polar opposite to the stark contrast of *us*. Some do this out of lack of experience, others out of fear, and there are, of course, the knuckle-dragging philistines who do it out of sheer pig-headedness. A chronic lack of imagination. No matter the reason, when our views become polarized, we end up trapping ourselves in an Internal Prison of ignorance, and we reinforce the External Prison of structural inequality and privilege. All because of a lack of imagination.

For years psychologists have shown us that we diligently hold on to beliefs and we will fight with loved ones, friends, colleagues, and other parents at the playground to defend the idea that *we are right*. Groups of people are excluded, denied resources, and denied basic human rights, all based on our ardent belief that *we are right* (making them wrong). And no matter how much proof is shown to us, no matter how evidence-based that proof is, and no matter how many images and diagrams are included in the PowerPoint, we cannot accept that other people might be right if that means that we are wrong. We cannot tolerate the discomfort of being wrong, and so we impose certainty where there is none and tell ourselves intricate stories to justify these inaccuracies. As a result, it can be extremely hard to reach beyond the confines of our own imagination—and yet even when we do, we can remain trapped by the intolerance of others.

When Jackie came out to her parents as queer, they called her a sinner and prohibited her from talking about it again. "I don't want to hear about that filth," they would sneer at her. "And don't you dare bring a girl anywhere near this house." Her father was religious, and so every night he read Bible verses to her, all centered around condemnation and hell if she did not atone for her *sinful sexuality*. She dreaded going home from school but had nowhere else to be, so she would make excuses about extra homework so she could retreat to her bedroom.

Sometimes she would hear her mother sobbing in the next room, and in those moments she thought things could not get worse. She was wrong. Late one night, when her parents were at the movies, her brother invited friends over for drinks in the basement. As Jackie tried to do her homework, one of the friends crept upstairs and tried to make conversation with her. "I hear you like girls," he leered, swaying a little from the alcohol. She tried to ignore him, but he walked over and pulled her shoulder so she faced his waist. "I was speaking to you, bitch," he hissed. She froze, and from that moment her memory fades a little. But she can remember how cruel he sounded when he said, "You think you are better than me."

Jackie can piece together enough of the night to know that she was sexually assaulted.

During the weeks that followed, her parents could not understand why she was suddenly withdrawn. She refused to attend her usual sporting activities, and even her grades began to suffer. “What have you been playing at?” her father bellowed late one night, after the school had got in contact about some missing assignments. “Instead of paying attention at school, you’re filling your head with vile thoughts about girls, wasting your time, no doubt missing classes. You disgust me.”

Jackie had no voice to explain what had happened, and her brother continued to invite the friend over. Every time he arrived at the house, her mind would go blank. Sheer terror. He never tried anything again, but still she would flinch every time she heard a creak of the floorboards outside her bedroom door. She was no longer safe in her own home, if ever she had been. One cool winter night, after her parents were asleep, she packed what belongings she could fit into her backpack, including the stuffed giraffe she had held onto every night since her birth, and left the house to stay with one of her friends. She never returned to her family home. There are organizations such as Lambda Legal, the True Colors Foundation, and the Ali Forney Center, who tirelessly work with LGBTQ+ youth to try and rectify the damage caused by homophobic, biphobic, and transphobic families. But their resources are not infinite, and they can only help the people they know about. There is a dark shadow of unreported cases where LGBTQ+ youth remain trapped in a prison of abusive family members, and there is no one to help them.

LGBTQ+ youth are frequently subjected to physical, emotional, and sexual abuse, and often this is within their own home. Even more troubling, the abuse is often at the hands of family members, or people who are supposed to protect them (the police, for example). One in four teens who come out are forced to leave their homes, 68 percent of teens experience family rejection after coming out, and LGBTQ+ youth experience homelessness at a rate 120 percent more frequently than their non-LGBTQ+ peers according to True Colors United. In addition, Lambda Legal reports that between 20 and 40 percent of all homeless youth in the US are part of the LGBTQ+ community. According to research carried out in the UK in February 2022 and reported in the *Guardian*, "nearly one in three LGBTQ+ people have experienced abuse—ranging from verbal harassment to threats of homelessness and physical violence—by a relative, most often their own parents, with two-thirds of them aged under 18 when the abuse first occurred." In addition, "transgender and non-binary people surveyed experienced higher levels of abuse from family members (43%)."

As Alessi and Martin point out in "Intersection of Trauma and Identity," "coming out can be traumatic . . . when the experience involves the loss of support of one's family or religious community." Such a loss shatters three assumptions about the world, namely the "benevolence of the world, meaningfulness of the world, and a sense of self-worth."

To understand how this bleak picture has emerged, we need to understand why people cannot reach beyond the confines of their discriminatory views. I sometimes blame my personal bête noire, the concept of labeling, for the wide-ranging discrimination that we see in so many societies. After all, according to Gwendolyn Keita, PhD, former executive director of American Psychological Association's Public Interest Directorate, "humans are naturally motivated to categorize people and objects." Just look at any statistic and you see an attempt to lump people into categories, whether it be race and ethnicity, sexuality, gender identity, age group, or religion. We tend to need to make sense of things, and so we categorize and generalize, even though this often takes us way beyond any *sense* that can be made. However, Keita claims that "discrimination goes beyond that. Research shows that the attitudes of people who discriminate reflect a complex set of factors including their history, sociocultural practices, economic forces, sociological trends and the influence of community and family beliefs. Some of the most damaging forms of discrimination are the result of deep-seated, destructive generalizations about a certain group. In such cases, people harbor unrealistic, disparaging beliefs about a group and its members, while also believing in the moral or intellectual superiority of their own group. These individuals are consciously aware of their negative emotions toward members of the group, and intend to harm, disadvantage, or avoid them." Things can get extremely ugly when family members hold "unrealistic, disparaging beliefs" about their own family members. If it is the caregivers holding those "unrealistic, disparaging beliefs" about LGBTQ+ youths, it is no surprise that these young people end up experiencing abuse or homelessness. It is also no surprise that these groups suffer from higher rates of depression, anxiety, trauma, and suicide.

I can't tell you how many clients I have worked with who have tried to heal the trauma caused by discrimination. The Human Rights Watch published a report on the discrimination experienced by LGBTQ+ youth in US schools, and here are just some of the accounts:

- "My son was dragged down the lockers, called 'gay' and 'fag' and 'queer,' shoved into a locker, and picked up by his neck. And that was going on since sixth grade. They tried shoving him into a girls' bathroom and said that he's worthless and should be a girl."
- "My dad told me and my brother that if we ever come out to be gay, lesbian, or bisexual, we'll get disowned or kicked out of the house."
- (From a transgender child) "I started getting a lot of anonymous people telling me to kill myself, that it wasn't worth living. I called the school and told them what was going on and they didn't do anything."
- "People will ask really intrusive questions about your sex life when they find out you're a non-straight

woman. They ask questions you wouldn't ask anyone else."

- "A lot of what I did to be safe was to be even more outrageous. If I'm so queer that nobody will talk to me, they won't hurt me. I did things to make myself much more gay: play up my gay lisp, feminize my voice, feminize my speech, I had hella long pink hair. That was my thinking: Become such an outsider they won't even approach me."
- (When teachers use the wrong pronouns) "It was like a little mental pinch. It doesn't seem like a big deal, but eventually you bruise."

Discrimination is a form of trauma, and it can result in post-traumatic stress disorder (PTSD), as explained in "Intersection of Trauma and Identity." Symptoms of PTSD include hypervigilance (where you are constantly on alert for danger), flashbacks, avoidance (for example, avoidance of situations that might trigger you to reexperience the trauma, which can result in social withdrawal), a distorted sense of blame, a diminished interest in activities, difficulty sleeping, difficulty concentrating, and self-destructive behavior.

Things can get a great deal more complicated, and harmful, when that discrimination is perpetrated by someone's caregiver. Often this results in complex post-traumatic stress disorder (C-PTSD), which includes the symptoms of PTSD but also features complications in how survivors form relationships with other people. Discrimination perpetrated by caregivers is a deep severance of trust, and so it can be exceptionally hard for a survivor to trust anyone else to form a secure attachment. Survivors of C-PTSD also find it difficult to regulate their emotions, either shutting down completely or becoming flooded with overwhelming emotion. Survivors of C-PTSD can also carry intensely negative self-beliefs such as *I am worthless*, *I am unlovable*, or *I am unsafe.* For members of the LGBTQ+ community, particularly LGBTQ+ youth, there can be a sense of powerlessness, or a hopeless sense of being trapped between the risk of violence or estrangement if you come out, and the prospect of mental health challenges (stress, anxiety, and depression, for example) as you attempt to conceal your sexuality or true gender identity.

When I work with people who have experienced discrimination—on the basis of sexuality, gender identity, race, ethnicity, religion, neurodivergence, or disability—I find the challenges to mental health are not because of their identity but the lack of imagination, or the ignorance, of the perpetrators of discrimination. Charles Horton Cooley conceptualized the looking-glass self, which means that we view ourselves through the eyes of how others view us. If you grow up in a household where you are viewed as "sinful," "wrong," "dirty," or where others do not even see the real you, is it any wonder that your self-esteem can be crushed to the point of suicidal ideation, self-harm, or chronic depression?

**

Respite – How to recognize the symptoms of trauma that result from discrimination

Based on research, these are some of the trauma symptoms that result from discrimination:

- Hypervigilance (this means that you are constantly on alert, waiting for danger)
- Flashbacks
- Avoidance
- A distorted sense of blame
- A diminished interest in activities
- Difficulty sleeping
- Difficulty concentrating
- Self-destructive behavior
- A sense of powerlessness

- Hopelessness

**

In 1957, Leon Festinger introduced the concept of *cognitive dissonance*, stating that "the individual strives toward consistency within himself" and "there is the same kind of consistency between what a person knows or believes and what he does." When faced with facts that contradict the individual's beliefs—for example, if a caregiver discovers that a family member is part of the LGBTQ+ community—the individual can experience tension that they will try to reduce with cognitive games. For example, they will ignore facts about the harm of discrimination. Alternatively, they might interpret the facts in a selective manner, or criticize the facts as unfounded or based on unreliable data. They might even try to reinterpret the data in a way to claim that there is no discrepancy between the facts and their beliefs.

Related to this is *confirmation bias*, another example of how people find it hard to reach beyond the confines of their imagination. People tend to select evidence that only confirms their originals beliefs (bias), which helps them avoid the discomfort of cognitive dissonance.

The inconvenience of truth (and trust)

Often, we become polarized and discriminatory in our views because the truth, or verifiable facts, are inconvenient. We simply do not have the time to find out more and expand our imagination. It is a matter of evolution and survival that we cannot learn about every detail of everything. As a result, we need to rely on the knowledge of others. As Elizabeth Kolbert pointed out in her article in the *New Yorker*, "the Bronze Age wouldn't have amounted to much" if everyone had tried to master the principles of metalworking "before picking up a knife." We need to rely on the knowledge of others, and so we need to trust others.

"Countries with higher levels of trust tend to grow faster economically," Maria Konnikova wrote in *The Confidence Game,* and there is a "strong positive relationship between generalized trust, intelligence, health, and happiness." Our ability to trust each other and cooperate can be viewed as huge advantages; without these advantages we might not have evolved as much as we have. However, this evolution, this incessant *advancement*, has come at a cost. To trust and cooperate with each other, we must rely on the knowledge of others, but this knowledge might not be accurate. As a result, we run the risk of treating other people's knowledge as "fact," which turns into misinformation. In other words, instead of widening our imagination and comprehending the broad spectrum of life, we rely on half-baked knowledge from others or recycled, outmoded views.

Worse, even when we discover that these outmoded views amount to misinformation, we turn a blind eye to this inconvenient truth. Our emotions get in the way of accurate information, and as cognitive scientists Steven Sloman and Philip Fernbach put it, in *The Knowledge Illusion: Why We Never Think Alone*, "strong feelings about issues do not emerge from deep understanding."

Even when we find out that the misinformation might have been the work of a confidence artist, still we find it hard to widen our imagination enough to accept that we were wrong. One reason for this, according to Konnikova, is that we believe we deserve the benefit with which the con artist was luring us. This fits with the concept of "personal specialness" that we mentioned in Chapter 3. In *The Gift of Therapy*, Yalom claimed that we operate under a belief that "life will not deal with us in the same harsh way it deals with everyone else." We work hard and we are kind to our loved ones, so *surely* we do not deserve to fall victim to a confidence artist who spreads misinformation for some sort of gain. As a result, we might refuse to broaden our imagination and choose to hold onto the misinformation that the confidence artist sold us. You only have to think of the misinformation spread by a former president of the United States to understand how people's emotions can leave them in a state of perpetual denial. It was astounding to see the amount of cognitive dissonance and confirmation bias these followers deployed to protect his ego and power base. It would have been quite the spectacle—almost entertaining—if it had not resulted in so much misery and heartache for so many.

We are so enamored with our own views that we will hold onto them at the expense of friends, family members, our career, and sometimes even our life. In *Dying for Ideas: The Dangerous Lives of the Philosophers*, Costica Bradatan offers the examples of Socrates, Hypatia, Giordano Bruno, Thomas More and Jan Patočka, who all sacrificed their lives rather than relinquish the beliefs they held so dear. And we can see plenty of examples of people in the twenty-first century who are determined to hold on to ideas that fly in the face of reason, no matter how much scientific proof is offered. The trouble is that science appeals to the rational mind while our ideas, our viewpoint, make up our identity. Often our identity has been created amongst people we care about—family or friends. As a result, our identity appeals to our emotions. We *feel* a sense of belonging. To challenge some of our beliefs might be to challenge that sense of belonging, and that can be deeply painful; in some cases, it can even be destabilizing.

Our craving for quick fixes in an Insta-Tok age

To reach beyond the confines of our imagination, we need to resist the temptation for a quick fix. Reaching for the half-baked arguments that overlook other people's experiences is all too easy and inevitably leaves us more polarized than before. For every limited view one way, there is an equally simplistic view to the polar opposite. The war in Ukraine, the COVID pandemic, the Supreme Court's decision to overturn Roe v Wade, the election of certain presidents in the United States, and countless other issues have continued to create division amongst family members, friends, work colleagues, and even nations. Polarized thinking is similar to what cognitive behavioral therapists call *all-or-nothing thinking* or *black-and-white thinking*. When we adopt this way of thinking, we tend to use absolute and generalizing statements, with no room for ambiguity nor circumstances to consider. It is just right or wrong. If you are a survivor of trauma, you may find that you slip into the use of this way of thinking more often-- understandably, because the trauma you experienced once left you powerless or overwhelmed, no doubt with an intense fear for any ambiguity. The trouble is, when we cut corners and go for the quick fix of black-and-white perspectives, we run the risk of bypassing information that might help us with a long-term solution to our problems.

This Insta-Tok age of quick flicks through photos and videos has created a fertile breeding ground for short-circuited thinking. Ever since someone thought it would be cool to share a photo online, the chicken or egg debate has been raging about whether polarization or social media came first. But when a bear enters your backyard and poses a threat to your children, you don't stand around debating with your neighbors about who forgot to shut the gate. No matter how this polarization started, we need to address the threat that it poses to our young. Those who wish to polarize our society understand the value of targeting young and malleable minds, and social media giants have a responsibility to monitor this. The trouble is, these are the same social media giants that are intent on maximizing their profits, and some news outlets claim these giants are targeting children as young as six years old. When we see what little regulation there is to the information (and misinformation) that is circulated at the speed of light, this trend is extremely worrying.

The witch-hunt

As easy as it would be to blame polarization and discrimination on the advent of this Insta-Tok age, we can trace the black-and-white thinking of polarized views to sometime between 628 and 551 BCE (BC). Rachel Christ-Doane, Director of Education at the Salem Witch Museum, points out in *Witches: Evolving Perceptions* that it was during this period the Iranian prophet Zoroastrian introduced the concept of dualism, a belief that good and evil are separate. Until then, polytheistic religions prevailed, allowing for a belief that there is good and evil, black and white, in all of us. With the introduction of dualism, however, it became far easier for our views to be polarized because we were no longer just trying to argue that we were right. We were right*eous*. We became the pure, the chosen ones who could sit in judgment over the *others*, making a *them* in contrast with *us*, so *they* can serve as a container for all the evil, all the pain and suffering; the bad in contrast with our goodness. Fast forward about seven hundred years to the 1400s and we find people being burned at the stake in Europe, or hanged in England, for being a witch. Not only were we polarizing each other, painting some people as *bad* so we could proclaim our goodness, we were executing them under this pretense. And because we were righteous, we were doing it to protect ourselves and others. *Think of the children*, we no doubt exclaimed, instantly legitimizing our hatred and condemnation by appealing to our most base emotions. The righteous grew stronger and disempowered the wrongdoers by creating a cause out of polarization. We claimed that we had to do it, that we had no choice, as legitimate an argument as self-defense (the politicians of the twenty-first century continue to do this today). By the 1600s, these polarizing concepts were washing up on the shorelines of the East Coast. In 1648 Margaret Jones was hanged in Boston, accused of being a witch when in reality her only crime was *difference*. Difference was a crime if you were unmarried or elderly, or if your belief system did not match the belief system of the majority. Healers and midwives, for example, were targeted as witches.

In patriarchal societies such as the United States and England, it is no coincidence that women were the majority of those targeted as different—so different that they were accused of being witches. In 1486 Heinrich Kramer wrote a book called *Malleus Maleficarum*, that was, in effect, a self-help guide to hunting witches. In it he proclaimed that women were more likely to be tempted into witchcraft because of "their inherent moral and rational deficits." Now, centuries later, it is still women who are the subject of persecution. It took years to get anywhere when it comes to recognizing their equal rights and still they suffer. As I wrote this book, the United States Supreme Court overturned Roe v. Wade, a 1973 Supreme Court decision that recognized a woman's right to abortion as protected by the Constitution. A group of mainly Roman Catholic straight, white, cisgender men decided to put the lives of millions of women across the United States at risk by denying them the Constitutional right to an abortion. Women's lives will be decided by the political point-scoring legislatures of each state, some of which have made it clear that they will make no exceptions to allow an abortion for someone who has been raped or whose life is threatened by the pregnancy or birth. But this is not just a persecution of women. Just as the pandemic hit certain communities harder than others, so too will the Supreme Court decision hit certain women harder than others. According to Dr Jamila Taylor, director of health care reform at The Century Foundation, the hardest hit by the overturning of Roe v. Wade will be low-income women of color. It is the dawn of the twenty-first century witch-hunt, where polarization, division, and discrimination continue to thrive.

Scapegoating

Polarization thrives on difference, and when people appear different, they become the object of blame. The concept of scapegoating has been extensively discussed in the context of family systems and group dynamics, and we have also seen a world leader blame certain groups for the leader's own prejudices and sense of inadequacy. To preserve a family system, an individual family member is often targeted and labeled "problematic" or "troublesome." The scapegoat. The black swan of George, whom we met in Chapter 3, became the scapegoat of the family after his mother's abuse. What was clearly symptoms of post-traumatic stress disorder (PTSD) was, to George's sister and father, bewildering behavior that warranted the labels of "problematic" and "troublesome" that they were attaching to him. They could not understand why George was so disruptive to the family, veering from outbursts of anger to distant, flat-faced moments of (what they thought was) indifference. Throughout all of this, George's mother watched on in silence, allowing her son to be pushed further out of the family. Eventually George's sister cut all contact with him, unwilling to let him play a part in the new family she was creating with her boyfriend.

Scapegoating can become a self-fulfilling prophecy where the designated target reacts to this familial alienation by acting out. In a futile attempt to right the balance, or heal their pain, the scapegoat can argue with the family members, or they might turn to alcohol or drugs to cope with the pain of this alienation. The family then has more reason to reject this scapegoat, pointing to the *evidence* that this family member is, indeed, problematic, and should be shunned. In a very utilitarian way, the scapegoat is treated this way to preserve the balance of the family or group as a whole, becoming the sacrificial black sheep of the family. Some believe that we are not simply finding a scapegoat to preserve the family or group, but also to project our own shame or sense of wrongdoing. We project our "shadow" onto the scapegoat, making them a container for "the thing a person has no wish to be," as described by Jung in *Collected Works of C.G. Jung.*

During the COVID pandemic, we saw scapegoating in its most vile form as we witnessed a rise in attacks on Asian

Americans and Pacific Islanders. Stop AAPI Hate is a coalition that "tracks and responds to incidents of hate, violence, harassment, discrimination, shunning, and child bullying against Asian Americans and Pacific Islanders in the United States." According to their report, since the pandemic "a total of 10,905 hate incidents against Asian American and Pacific Islander (AAPI) persons were reported to Stop AAPI Hate," with 4,632 cases occurring in 2020 (42.5%) and 6,273 occurring in 2021 (57.5%). Polarized views, intolerance, and violence go hand in hand with epidemics and pandemics, and you only need to look to the cholera epidemics between the 1830s and 1860s to see evidence of this. In that case, the Irish immigrants bore the brunt. Later, during the HIV/AIDS epidemic, members of the LGBTQ+ community were the scapegoats, and even today, the LGBTQ+ community are the scapegoats for the current 2022 monkeypox outbreak.

**

Respite – Scapegoating

Signs that you, or another member of your group (family, coworkers, or friendship group, for example) have become the scapegoat:

- You are frequently blamed for things that go wrong within the group
- You are told that you are "overly sensitive" or "imagining things"
- You are labeled "the troublemaker" or "problematic"
- Members of your group frequently speak badly about you behind your back
- Members of your group act in an abusive or hostile manner, and other members are complicit in their silence
- Members of your group try to isolate you from the group

- You have become estranged from the group, and you do not know why

**

Empathy (or *Stop being an ahole*)**

When we are confined to a limited imagination or experience, we end up blind to the pain of others, and so we suffer from a fundamental lack of empathy. Someone does not care about the lady who is shivering in the rain and begging for spare change because that someone has a roof over his head and a working heating system. Someone else does not care when someone is called a racial slur because she lives in an area where she assumes that everyone is of the same racial or ethnic background. He laughs at someone who has a panic attack when they are in the elevator because he has never been afraid of heights. She is confused why someone won't hand in a project on time because his wife just died because she has never experienced the death of a loved one.

Empathy is an ability to step into someone else's shoes and see the world from their perspective. For example, if someone hits their head, you can see that they might feel pain, and you can imagine that pain. It seems so simple, and yet it is a skill that is so easily forgotten in the heat of the moment. As mental health practitioners make their living trying to understand the emotions of other people, empathy is an essential part of the job, and most would point to Carl Rogers as the most notable psychologist who emphasized the importance of empathy in a therapeutic relationship. There are various scales to measure empathy in the therapeutic relationship (for example, Robert Carkhuff, George Gazda, and Allen E. Ivey). Most therapists agree that without empathy, the therapeutic endeavor becomes an argument in semantics, or a patronizing exercise of sympathy imposed from the lofty heights of an "expert" therapist. Empathy serves as a leveler between therapist and client, ensuring that the client remains at the center of the work, as both expert on their own worldview and the agent for change.

Just as the pandemic revealed polarized views concerning mask mandates and vaccines, we also have the polar opposite perspective on the importance of empathy from psychologists such as Paul Bloom, who blame empathy for producing "parochial" and "bigoted" results where "emotions distort reality." Bloom claims that when we focus too much on empathy, we can pay too much attention to the individual at the expense of social issues. I can understand Bloom's concerns—particularly when you look at criticisms leveled against psychodynamic therapists who, some argue, focus too much on the individual without an appreciation of the social structures that create much of the suffering of their individual clients. However, I know many therapists of varying disciplines who attach great importance to the role of empathy in their work, but who are also well aware of the structural inequalities that create and perpetuate the suffering endured by their clients. Perhaps the answer is that empathy is essential, but it is not a panacea, and if we have any hope of helping our clients, we cannot forget the social structures within which each individual lives.

If we are to reach beyond our confines, we need to see that we can exist in a different way, that our identity does not depend on these outmoded or irrational examples of misinformation. With courage, we can push past the discomfort of *not knowing*, and widen our imagination to the possibility that there is much more to life than what we thought we knew. Only then can we have the hope for growth and freedom. The trouble is, no matter how much we hope for this, there will always be someone who tries to imprison us with their intolerance or discrimination.

If we are to be free, we need to learn:

How can we manage when others reach beyond our boundaries?

CHAPTER 7

Beyond our boundaries

No one can make you feel inferior without your consent.
- Eleanor Roosevelt

No matter how many times I asked them to stop, she kept calling me by my deadname. She claimed she forgot so I let it slide, but then later during the meal, when she turned to the waiter, she started to misgender me. You could see the confusion on the waiter's face as they looked from me to my Mom and back again. It was humiliating.

This was not an isolated incident. It had been years since Logan had come out, and still his mother chose to deadname and misgender her son. There were heated arguments when Logan's mother would scream obscenities after yet another night of drinking; and at one point she called her son "an abomination." It was seven in the evening, and she had been drinking with colleagues since lunchtime, so her words were slurred as she said "God made you a *girl*, and nothing you ever say will convince me otherwise. You are trying to take my daughter from me, and I will not let you do it."

For years Logan tried to make the relationship work. No matter the abuse, he wanted to introduce some type of family to whomever he eventually fell in love with, and his mother was all he had. But after repeated attempts to keep the peace, he started to feel torn apart inside every time he was around her.

No matter how much you try to reach beyond the confines of your imagination, or the imagination of others, no matter how much you try to empathize or collaborate, someone will still push beyond your boundaries. There will be times when you decide that someone has encroached on your personal space or acted in a way that is abusive (verbally, physically, or emotionally), and that you need to rebuild those trampled boundaries. Since the pandemic, we have had an increased awareness of boundaries and personal space. When news of COVID-19 first broke, most people were too scared to ignore the health advisories, but as time went on, a division emerged between people who wore a mask and people who refused to, or people who kept a distance of six feet from others and people who dismissed the health measures with suspicion. Suddenly we were faced with a tricky dilemma where some claimed that it was an encroachment of their boundary for anyone to demand that they wear a mask, and yet others claimed that noncompliance encroached on other people's boundaries by exposing their health to undue risk. This summed up a dilemma that has existed since time immemorial: How can we negotiate, construct, and enforce boundaries when they do not coincide, when our boundaries may be viewed as an encroachment of other people's boundaries? We cannot zealously protect our autonomy with all the ferocity of a rottweiler and turn a blind eye to the boundaries of other people. That is unsustainable if we do not wish to live in a world of perpetual conflict. We forget all too easily how intimate our relationship is with the world in which we live. According to Kabat-Zinn in *Meditation is Not What You Think*, there is a "give-and-take of that relationality" that continually shapes our lives. When we forget this, when we become "insensitive to the ways our lives actually impinge upon and shape the world and the ways in which the world shapes our lives in a symbiotic dance of reciprocity and interdependence on every level," we isolate ourselves "from our own possibilities."

Since the pandemic, this dilemma has been particularly distressing for parents of school-aged (and younger) children. Many have struggled with the impossible task of balancing the need for their children to remain healthy with the need to keep their children educated and socialized. Take Abigail, for example. She always made friends easily, but when she entered third grade and the pandemic hit, her parents stopped her playdates. As she progressed into fourth grade, Abigail and her parents could see how differently other families were treating the pandemic, and they agonized over what was the right decision regarding playdates. Eventually they decided to let Abigail play with her friends unrestricted, but she refused to. When her mother, Dana, pressed her for more information, Abigail broke down in tears and said, “Everyone hates me.” It turned out that there were a handful of children who were criticizing everything about Abigail, from the way she dressed, talked, and even walked. Even worse, they would make other children in the class laugh at Abigail whenever she walked to the front of the class. She had tried to keep her schoolmates happy in a bid to make them stop, but nothing seemed to work; they still chose to pick on her. “I never want to go back to school,” Abigail sobbed into her mother’s chest. Dana’s initial thought was anger—not directed at the other children, but towards the parents and teachers who were no doubt allowing this to happen. She knew that this was just the blood-pumping fight-or-flight response of her sympathetic nervous system, so she started to breathe deeply, lengthening her outward breath a little longer to regain her composure. Then, having climbed the ladder of her autonomic nervous system back up to the *social engagement system* of her ventral vagal pathway, she was able to connect with her daughter and support her in a more nurturing way.

Abigail felt safe as she glanced up to her mother’s softened eyes. “What should I do?” she asked, wiping away her tears. “Well, you did an excellent thing by telling me,” Dana smiled, brushing the hair out of her daughter’s face. She wanted to tell her daughter how much pain she felt when she heard her daughter's account, and how it felt like those crass children were trampling a precious flower with their big muddy boots. But she knew that any imagery of vulnerability was not going to help because the last self-image Abigail needed was helplessness or fragility.

"I would love to fix this for you. I would love to go and talk to those children about kindness, and how hurtful words and actions can be. I would also like to speak to their parents and the teachers, but all of this would be taking away from all the things *you* could do. And if I step in and try and sort this for you, I will deprive you of the chance to learn how to resolve something like this next time. Because unfortunately, there will be a next time, and a next, and a next after that. There are plenty of people who can be mean, or who encroach on our boundaries, and we need to learn what to do in those situations."

It is so easy to jump in and try to take the pain away from our children. But Dana did the right thing. She went on to explain to her daughter about relationship conflict, assertiveness, and the importance of boundaries. She helped her daughter see that it is impossible to please everyone all the time. She urged her daughter to trust her intuition about who she continued to play with and who to spend less time around.

Eventually Abigail is going to have to feel the burn and discomfort of conflict; there is no way to avoid this. Others might try to use Abigail's kindness as a weapon, but no amount of appeasement is going to protect her from this. Only boundaries will help.

Boundaries define the parameters of our needs and feelings. When we respect our own boundaries, and we enforce those boundaries around other people, we are more likely to get our needs met, and we are more likely to have our feelings respected. But it isn't all about us. A healthy approach to boundaries strikes a balance between our own needs and feelings, and the needs and feelings of others. This makes strategic sense because to evolve we need to *collaborate* with each other. Without a sense of someone else's needs and feelings, and a respect for their boundaries, this collaboration is doomed to fail.

Research into neural plasticity shows that positive social interaction actually changes the brain, helping us with empathy, improved behavior, and improved cognition. You don't have to love or even like everyone, but you need to continuously search for that small corner of overlap where you share something in common, or you each feel like the other is at least getting something in return. If we don't consider the needs of others, we can end up stepping on the toes of someone who might mean us harm. Getting along means continually assessing how protective we must be of our needs in any given moment and how much we can sacrifice for the sake of someone else's needs. Your boundaries are dividing lines that determine the extent to which you reach beyond your confines to strengthen your core, running the risk of encroaching on someone else's boundaries, and when you choose to remain within your confines and respect another person's boundaries. We can learn a great deal about boundaries when we learn about how we securely attach to other people.

A boundary that is securely attached

Sophia hated it when her boyfriend left for the weekend. Louis had relatives in Pennsylvania, and he would be gone from Friday until late Sunday afternoon, so it left little time together before they were each busy with their working week. "You could hang out with your friends," he would tell her, but this only made her feel worse, and she started to wonder whether he was just trying to find a way to avoid her. Distressed, she started calling and texting him more frequently. Her heart would stop after she sent each text message, knowing she sounded desperate, and then she would stare at the phone until she received a reply. The time between each message started to get shorter, and she started to demand that he share more and more of what he was doing.

Eventually Louis said, "Look, I need space, okay?" She took this as the end of her relationship, and, devastated, she turned up at her mother's house in floods of tears.

Sophia was showing signs of an *anxious attachment style*, where she was favoring contact with her boyfriend (in other words, *intimacy*) at the expense of any independence they might enjoy in this relationship. We learn our attachment styles early on, from the years when we attach to our caregivers. When you show signs of anxious attachment, you become distressed when you are not in contact with your loved one, and you question whether they still love you because you, in effect, believe that when you are out of their sight, you are out of their mind.

The anxious attachment style is in stark contrast to an *avoidant attachment style*, where you value independence over contact (or intimacy) with your loved one. As a result, you might call or visit less, or you shut down your emotions in the face of conflict. There is also a *disorganized* style of attachment—a confusing mixture of anxious attachment and avoidant attachment, resulting in craving contact with your beloved one minute, and avoiding them the next.

The ideal style of attachment is *secure attachment,* a healthy balance of independence but also contact (or *intimacy*) with your loved one. When they are out of sight, you are content that you are not out of their mind, and you settle into this contentment because you trust them. The secure style of attachment can help you to enforce healthy boundaries in a relationship, keeping a balance between contact with each other, and your own independence.

Although you learn your style of attachment at an early age, with your caregivers, you can strive for this ideal form of attachment in friendships as well as romantic relationships. In *The Art of Happiness*, HH Dalai Lama and Howard C. Cutler explain that we need to expand our understanding of what constitutes intimacy. Too often we associate intimacy with a romantic relationship, or a significant other, but the Dalai Lama and Cutler explain that intimacy can be enjoyed with many people. Already we are "surrounded by friends, family, or acquaintances – relationships that could easily be cultivated into genuine and deeply satisfying intimate relationships . . . The Dalai Lama's model of intimacy is based on a willingness to open ourselves to many others, to family, friends, and even strangers, forming genuine and deep bonds based on our common humanity." However, without a respect for boundaries, this genuine and deep bond is impossible.

**

Respite – Different forms of attachment

We learn our attachment styles from a young age, often from our caregivers. Even though these patterns are formed early on, they can be changed:

- Secure attachment – You value independence as much as you value intimacy. You have trust in the relationship so when you are out of each other's sight, you are not necessarily out of each other's mind.
- Anxious attachment – You value intimacy at the expense of independence. You close the gap between each moment of contact with the other person, sharing too much, and making them feel suffocated.
- Avoidant attachment – You value independence at the expense of intimacy. There are longer periods of time in between each moment of contact, and you share less, making people feel isolated from you.
- Disorganized attachment – You fluctuate between anxious and avoidant attachment, sometimes craving intense contact, and then avoiding the person altogether. Often this results in confusion and frustration for everyone involved.

**

Assertiveness, the key to healthy boundaries

If only Sophia could have explained herself. If she had shared with Louis how scared she was of losing him, instead of demanding so much from him, he might have understood. Assertive communication can help establish secure attachment, and both, in turn, can help you to maintain the security of healthy boundaries.

If you are unsure how to identify assertiveness and distinguish it from aggressive or passive behavior, simply construct this sentence: "I feel [*insert emotion*] because of [*insert reason for that emotion*]." This is an example of assertive communication. You don't need to over-explain yourself; often the more concise the better. Make sure you keep calm, which may require breathing exercises, mindfulness, or meditation. Then, if there is any confusion or opposition, simply repeat your simple sentence of assertive communication. "I feel [*insert emotion*] because of [*insert reason for that emotion*]."

In *Set Boundaries, Find Peace*, Nedra Glover Tawwab reminds us that we need to speak up about our boundaries because "boundaries are not unspoken rules." There is no point sitting in silence about an apparent boundary incursion when the person never knew where your boundary was in the first place. Yet as much as we should be communicative when it comes to boundaries, we also need to be flexible. Circumstances change, and as a result, we often must process new information and explore new comfort zones.

Before I had children, I had a very different set of comfort zones. I tolerated far less in terms of mistakes, and I had as much patience as a cat on a hot tin roof. However, for the sake of my children, I have reconfigured my life and my boundaries. Without this flexibility, parenting would have been a disaster. When I work with parents who claim they are too busy to learn new skills (*Can't teach an old dog new tricks*), they do not understand how simple assertiveness can be. Either that or they don't appreciate the adverse consequences of lacking assertiveness. When we lack assertiveness, and we allow our boundaries to be continuously encroached, we set an unhealthy example for our children. If our children don't learn about assertiveness and the enforcement of boundaries, how can they manage tricky situations such as manipulative friendships, gossiping, bullying, dating abuse, and peer pressure to engage in risky behavior such as alcohol and substance misuse? Studies show that children who learn about assertiveness and boundaries learn to accept personal responsibility, they have a better sense of self-esteem, and they are better equipped to enjoy healthy, balanced relationships.

But acting as a role model for our children goes further than just assertiveness and boundaries. As Don Miguel Ruiz explained in *The Four Agreements: A Practical Guide to Personal Freedom*, you also need to "be impeccable with your word," take nothing personally, avoid making assumptions, and always do your best.

Caring for yourself enough to rebuild those boundaries

To rebuild the boundaries that someone has encroached, you must recognize the importance of those boundaries. In the face of opposition, others can easily make us feel like we are being obstructive or uncaring. This is where we need to care for ourselves. Even though so much of our upbringing, and the way society is shaped, suggests that we should not prioritize our own feelings or needs, this is an essential key to freedom from within.

To help with this, I appreciate the wisdom from Tawwab: "There is always someone out there whose standards you aren't meeting," and we will quickly burn out if we try to appease everyone. Dana helped Abigail to see this, but adults also need to be reminded of this. We can become parents, we can become in-laws, we can fulfill a professional role, and each of these carries a whole set of expectations of us. The trouble is that everyone has a different interpretation of those expectations. Take comfort in guiding yourself with a consistent set of values of your own creation, and take comfort from Tawwab's advice that "You can't please everyone, because everyone's needs are different."

Caring for yourself involves an analysis of the support you already have and the gaps you need to fill. Even when we have support networks in place, we sometimes need a little help with reaching out for that support. When I work with people, I often ask them who in their life they *would* turn to in a crisis, and then I ask them who they *have* turned to. Rarely do the two lists correlate. We don't reach out, or we can't, because we fear judgment. Or we assume they are too busy, or their problems are a great deal worse than ours. Instead, our focus is on others, and we wouldn't think twice about offering other people the support that we deny ourselves.

Caring for yourself can also include recognizing the difference between supporting someone and rescuing them. It feels good to support people, and sometimes it is a noble pursuit. But when the support becomes a rescue, we place ourselves in a hierarchical position over them. When we do this, we overlook any strength or resources they have to rescue themselves, and we run the risk of encroaching on their boundaries. Although we believe we have good reason to act, doing this out of fear or some other emotion can distort our judgment. Instead of managing those emotions by acting on them and jumping into the role of rescuer, we should learn to regulate our emotions by, for example, engaging in mindful breathing to calm our amygdala and allow our prefrontal cortex to get involved in the decision-making process. This might enable us to weigh the potential risks and benefits of getting involved.

Marie adored her girlfriend because Talia had been the first person who had ever shown any interest in her. Her parents were too busy with a business venture to take any notice of her loneliness, and her brother used to call her hurtful, homophobic names. So to find a safe and accepting place in Talia was a dream come true. They met during their final year of high school, and at the time, Talia was drinking heavily in between classes. Maria helped her girlfriend start a rehab program, and Talia managed to abstain from alcohol. As soon as they graduated high school, they started living together while they attended a local college. However, after two years of a pandemic and all the uncertainty that had introduced, they were fighting on a daily basis, and Talia had started to drink again. Maria told herself that she could solve Talia's drinking problem, and even though Talia had refused to attend rehab, Maria devised a number of different covert strategies to trick her into various alcohol programs and interventions. Each time Talia found out about Maria's tricks, she became enraged and threw the furniture around the apartment, and each time Maria would back down because she was frightened of what Talia might do to both of them. Late one night Maria's fight with Talia got ugly, and Talia slammed her against the wall and punched her several times in the stomach. Still tasting blood, Maria ran to the house of an old school friend.

"You deserve more than this, Maria," her friend Ezekiel told her.

"But she doesn't mean it," Maria insisted. "She has been under so much stress with the company making cuts, and if she loses this job, I don't know what she is going to do. She won't be able to afford college, and I know she wants to become a graphic designer. I don't know what to do, Ezekiel."

"What you need to do is stop all of this. You can't rescue her and stick around like her punching bag. Ultimately this is her mess to clear up. She had no right to lay her hands on you. You are in a relationship not a dictatorship."

"But she is so stressed, she really doesn't mean it."

"No one really does. But that is something she is going to have to figure out herself, and preferably with some professional help. You are not responsible for her rages, and you are not responsible for her drinking. You can't trick her into anything; she needs to accept professional help knowingly and willingly."

Slowly Maria accepted that she could not rescue Talia. If her girlfriend was going to recover, she would have to do it herself, with *professional* help. Maria also knew violence was unacceptable, so she moved out of the home she shared with her girlfriend. She still loved Talia, but she realized that they had lost sight of a balanced relationship, one where partners respected each other's boundaries and respected each other's feelings and needs.

Disengagement

If your boundaries are encroached, there is the option to disengage, and this can take many different forms. People often assume I mean separation or divorce, but you can disengage from someone by sharing less, or you can see them less often, or for shorter amounts of time. A useful guide to disengagement in all its forms is *Stop Walking on Eggshells* by Paul Mason and Randi Kreger. Although it was intended as advice for anyone living with someone with borderline personality disorder (BPD), the principles are useful advice for anyone who has had their boundaries encroached.

If you are experiencing abuse, there is also the option of getting in contact with the National Domestic Violence Hotline at https://www.thehotline.org/ or 1-800-799-SAFE. If you know a child who may need help, there is the Child Welfare Information Gateway at https://www.childwelfare.gov/ .

Sometimes it is hard to identify the signs of abuse, especially when you have been living with it for a long time. It can be particularly hard to recognize abuse when the perpetrator is your caregiver, some other family member, or your partner. Abusive behavior often involves an imbalance of power in which someone uses that power to control you.

Abuse can take many different forms, including physical or sexual abuse, verbal or emotional abuse, financial abuse, or isolation. Abuse can also include someone humiliating you, belittling you, calling you unkind names, dismissing your feelings or thoughts, threatening or using violence, or harassing you with unwanted contact (in the form of in-person visits, but also on social media, telephone calls, text messages, or emails). In her book *The Emotionally Abusive Relationship: How to Stop Being Abused and How to Stop Abusing*, psychotherapist Beverly Engel describes emotional abuse as "any nonphysical behavior or attitude that is designed to control, subdue, punish, or isolate another person through the use of humiliation or fear." Although some might try to minimize the harm of emotional abuse, it is important to know that emotional abuse is often the first stage of a cycle that leads to physical abuse. I have worked with too many people, and known people personally, who found this out the hard way. It is also important to be aware of the correlation between adverse childhood experiences (ACE) and abuse in adulthood. Research shows that the greater the number of adverse childhood experiences during childhood, the greater likelihood of poor "intergenerational cycles of ACE-related mental health, behavioral, and social problems," according to "Adverse Childhood Experiences and Health in Adulthood in a Rural Population-Based Sample." In other words, you may decide to tolerate abusive behavior from a partner but if your children are witnessing this, they are learning that they too must tolerate abuse, and the cycle will continue. Sometimes it helps to know that breaking this cycle is not just about your own needs, but an act to save future generations. Some people need to hear this additional benefit because their self-esteem has been chipped away by the abuse, making it feel impossible to take steps to disengage simply for their own sake.

It can be exceptionally hard to disengage from abusive behavior when you are trapped in a system where you must see the perpetrator every day. According to a report published by the American Association of University Women (AAUW), "more than 11% of all students experienced rape or sexual assault, and only 20% of female students who experienced sexual assault reported it to the authorities." In addition, "56% of girls in grades 7 to 12 had experienced sexual harassment at school, and 37% of those girls were unwilling to go to school as a result." The University of Illinois published the results of a five-year study of children from middle school to high school, and it was poignant that it was published in the same year that Brandy Vela, an eighteen-year-old from Texas City, shot herself in front of her family after years of bullying and sexual harassment. The study found that 21 percent of students reported "having been touched, grabbed, or pinched in a sexual way" and that many of the students were "dismissive of these experiences, even though they described them as very upsetting."

Dorothy Espelage, professor of education at the University of North Carolina, points out that adults are letting these children down when it comes to protecting their boundaries. One reason for this is that the parents (and sometimes even the teachers) lack knowledge about steps that should and can be taken in response to sexual harassment and bullying. For example, Stop Sexual Assault In Schools (SSAIS), a US 501 (c)(3) nonprofit created "to address sexual harassment/assault and K-12 students' rights" states that "most K-12 schools, parents, and students are not aware of how Title IX relates to sexual harassment/assault in schools. For example, many wonder why schools should investigate student sexual assaults at all and not simply leave the matter to the police." As SSAIS point out, "Title IX is a civil rights law. It prohibits all educational institutions that receive federal money from discriminating against students on the basis of sex. Sexual harassment/assault is a form of discrimination because it can limit or prevent a student from participating in and benefiting from a school's educational program." SSAIS makes freely available resources to advise people of their rights pursuant to

Title IX, should a child experience harassment, so it is worth a read: https://stopsexualassaultinschools.org/know-your-rights/.

The Department of Education has also created a checklist for schools to follow in order to adopt a comprehensive approach to harassment: https://www2.ed.gov/about/offices/list/ocr/checklist.html.

**

Respite – Different forms of abuse

Although abuse is commonly associated with physical violence, abuse can also be emotional verbal, sexual, financial, and isolation. It is important to identify abuse in all its forms because research shows that emotional abuse can often lead to physical abuse. Emotional abuse can include:

- Humiliation
- Belittling
- Using unkind names
- Dismissing your feelings
- Unwanted contact including telephone calls, texts, emails, and messages on social media
- Invasion of your privacy
- Threats of harm
- Threats of abandonment
- Intimidation
- "Any nonphysical behavior or attitude that is designed to control, subdue, punish, or isolate another person through the use of humiliation or fear" (Beverly Engel)

**

When we effectively maintain our boundaries, and when we are free of undue coercion or control of others, we have autonomy. But what does this really mean? It is all very well having an open prison door, but if we do not recognize it, we are no less free.

How can we identify autonomy?

CHAPTER 8

What is beyond your confines? Autonomy?

I am no bird; and no net ensnares me;
I am a free human being with an independent will.
- *Jane Eyre*, Charlotte Bronte

If you are to reach beyond the confines of an Internal Prison, what are you reaching for? If you are not confined, you can act freely and make choices for yourself. In other words, you have *autonomy*. According to Erik Erikson, at between eighteen months and three years old, toddlers start negotiating the fine balancing act of autonomy and dependence, or autonomy versus shame. If a child successfully develops past this stage, they can make choices about the food they eat and the clothes they wear, and they show greater independence when it comes to bathroom rituals. The basic virtue to come out of all of this is free will, but the quest for autonomy does not just stop at this early age.

As we grow, we continue to negotiate more independence from our peers, and we might escape from imprisoning messages from our childhood or equally imprisoning thought patterns. But after all of that, we might still find that we are sacrificing our freedom. Still confined, but this time by a prison imposed by someone else, we lack autonomy. We are someone else's puppet.

According to Christine A. Courtois and Julian D. Ford in *Treatment of Complex Trauma*, autonomy is a person's "right to freedom of action and choice without being placed in a position of dependency" or "undue external control or coercion." Without free will we can end up losing our sense of self, becoming prisoners of other people's wishes or commands. Intimate relationships are a breeding ground for this sort of *dependency, undue external control*, and *coercion.* How many times have we put up with more than we should have because we were in love, or hoped that the relationship would improve, or had joint commitments such as a home or children together. And shame serves as a locked steel door, a hopeless dead end just when we think that maybe, just maybe, we could make our escape. *What would our friends make of this, after all these years of us being known as a couple? There would be questions and insinuations, and gaps in knowledge filled by wild speculation* (because we cannot abide not knowing). *We would become the* failed relationship, *the* troubled marriage, *and fingers would be pointed.*

Would people claim to have known all along that she was always the difficult one, and he was never home, and she was controlling, and he was loose with his affection for anyone but his other half? Often the Internal Prison of our own fears and assumptions interlocks with the coercion and undue control of others, and we end up trapped—from without and from within.

"Paul tells me that he wants us to work together when we are working from home. He wants to keep an eye on me, so he knows I am really working rather than lazing around. I guess I don't mind because it keeps the peace. Better that than the screaming matches we used to get embroiled in."

My stomach always tensed when I heard these accounts from Jackie. I have witnessed the curled lip from her husband as he ordered her to "get a move on" as they left the room, and I have seen how quickly she jumped to action in response. He was a bully. According to her accounts, he would criticize her clothing, criticize how loudly she laughed, and he even threw insults like "schizo," "odd," and "weirdo." Hardly the loving, supportive partner that she wanted to come home to each night, and hardly the nurturing, supportive partner who would encourage autonomy in the person he is supposed to love.

What made things worse was that this sort of relationship was all Jackie had ever known. Her childhood had featured a mother who would throw similar insults at her, constantly reminding Jackie that she never really wanted her in the first place. When Jackie was slow to clear up after herself, and she tended to be steady paced with everything, even the way she spoke, her mother would slap her on the head with the back of her hand. Jackie spoke of ringing in her ears, even years later. When Jackie ended up hanging out with the wrong friends, and her grades started to suffer, Jackie's mother directed Jackie's stepfather to give her a "talking to." This ended up with more slaps on the back of her head when he thought that she was not listening. At sixteen years old, she was starting to lose track of things, and when Jackie described her inability to follow conversations, I thought of the shutdown response of her dorsal vagal pathway. She had no will left to fight or flee, and it certainly wasn't safe to connect.

Fifteen years into a marriage with Paul, and the same pattern had emerged. When Jackie was a child, it had been her mother and stepfather, and now it was her husband chipping away at her self-esteem, so that she was defenseless against any attack on her autonomy. An erosion of someone's autonomy can start as a slender vein of doubt, threading its way through a person's freedom with little questions about how they look, what they do, and who they are. There are cursory comments of dissent, the occasional disagreement—it is a slow process that is so subtle, you do not even notice the gaping chasm that has emerged, the dark hole of doubt that has left you toppling into dependence on the other person.

In Jackie's case, the relationship had started off well. In the early days, when Paul would pick her up from her mother's house in a big white car, she appreciated the attention. Her mother always told Jackie that she "wasn't the pretty type," so she thought she should feel grateful and overlook any reservations. And there were plenty of those. He never liked her talking too much, so he would hold his big hand up to silence her if she became "too excitable," as he put it. He also liked to tell her what to wear, always being careful that she didn't show too much, and he had endless feedback about how she should fashion her hair. Although she had a few firm friends when they first met, eventually he found fault with each of them, pointing to transgressions over the years that justified telling her to sever ties with each of them.

But the one thing she found comforting was his stature—all six feet of him towering over her barely five-foot stature. It made me cringe when he twice told me, grimacing, that he could hold her with one hand if he wanted to. This sounded like a threat more than something he was proud of. In *Trauma and* Recovery, psychiatrist Judith Herman explains that adult survivors of childhood trauma can desperately long for "nurturance and care" and, as a result "seek out powerful authority figures who seem to offer the promise of a special caretaking relationship." This might have explained Jackie's initial attraction to Paul, but the trouble is, this longing for nurturance and care from such a powerful authority figure or caretaker can make it difficult to "establish safe and appropriate boundaries with others," creating a threat to autonomy from within.

One hope for Jackie to break this cycle was for her to discover that not all relationships are like this. When people come to therapy, it can be the first time that they have experienced a relationship of respect for their autonomy. It can be the first time they learn about boundaries, or the validity of their emotions, or empathy, support, and unconditional positive regard. But when you have shaped a self-identity based on the distortion of other people's control and coercion, to step away from it, even for a brief therapeutic hour, can feel like a freefall into the abyss. If we take away the words, the will, the constant presence of someone else, what will fill that gap? Will we feel cold and exposed, will we crumble without that person there to hold us up, no matter how hard their grip chafes us to the bone? Jackie was starting to see the common thread that ran through her husband's behavior and the childhood she had experienced at the hands of her mother and stepfather. There was no room for her own free will, no recognition of her wishes, her feelings, or her needs. Warming herself on the compassion that a therapeutic relationship can offer, the full extent of Paul's duress was slowly starting to unfurl before her eyes. Her growing understanding of him was like a blooming flower, and she could finally see how much he had emasculated her. Jackie thought of all the times she had limited herself just to appease her husband's sense of inadequacy. She even declined a promotion because she would have joined a team comprising mostly men. The fumes of Paul's intense jealousy were starting to suffocate her, and yet she realized how much dependence he had demanded of her. She didn't even have a bank account that was solely her own.

In collaboration with the National Coalition Against Domestic Violence (NCADV), Kellie Lynch, PhD and TK Logan, PhD surveyed professionals who work with "survivors of gender-based violence across the United States." The results covered September and December 2020, and for that period 83.7% of respondents identified Intimate Partner Violence (IPV), 70.2% identified child abuse, and 60.2% identified sexual assault. In each case, this was a significant increase, and seemingly attributable to the pandemic.

According to Tedros Adhanom Ghebreyesus, PhD, World Health Organization Director-General, violence against women has been "endemic in every country and culture" for a very long time. However, the COVID-19 pandemic has made things significantly worse. According to a United Nations report published in November 2021, "245 million women and girls aged 15 years or over have been subjected to sexual and/or physical violence perpetrated by an intimate partner in the previous 12 months" and "1 in 4 women (23%) said that COVID-19 has made things worse in terms of how safe they feel at home." As a result, the United Nations call this a "shadow pandemic."

All of this is far from surprising, given the lack of services available during the pandemic for people in need, and some say these services have still not recovered. Support organizations, shelters, and social workers were all put under tremendous pressure, reduced to a bare minimum service, or suspended altogether. At the same time, we saw an increase in domestic conflict due to people living and working from home, trapping some people with their abusers, on top of the additional stressors of the loss of jobs and businesses, the closure of childcare facilities and schools, and an increase in deaths and illnesses. Relationships can come under a huge amount of strain when the people involved are living with a constant sense of vigilance. Who can forget the fear created at the start of the pandemic, when we knew little about the full extent of COVID, and vaccines were not available? For a long time, vaccines were not available for children under five in the United States, and for some countries they are not available for anyone of any age. All of this can create a constant sense of vigilance that activates the sympathetic nervous system, pushing up the blood pressure leaving us unable to rest, relax, or play.

On top of the present-day triggers activating our sympathetic nervous system and creating a general sense of hypervigilance, old trauma wounds can be poked by similar feelings of uncertainty. In that case, the amygdala takes over, lessening the likelihood that cool, calm logic and rational thought have a chance to navigate or mediate the storm. What we can see from all of this is that it is not easy to draw a dividing line between freedom, or autonomy, and its opposite, where you are confined by the faulty messages of your past, the coercive influence in the present, or the dizzying sense of emotion dysregulation.

Autonomy requires freedom from imprisoning messages from our past

To act freely, to reach for autonomy, we need self-awareness. We need to free ourselves from the confines of imprisoning messages from our past so we can see the present for what it is. This is especially difficult when we are searching for autonomy in our life while still haunted by adverse childhood experiences. Like the roots of a family tree growing tightly around our awareness, it can be hard to disentangle the different experiences. In some respects, there may be parallels or common threads running through each story, but a clear distinction remains: *That was then, and this is now.*

Back then, we were a child, and by virtue of this, we were vulnerable, we had less power, and we depended upon our caregivers for our survival. As psychiatrist Herman explains, when the perpetrator is a caregiver, there is a power imbalance, and often "the exercise of parental power is arbitrary, capricious, and absolute. Rules are erratic, inconsistent, or patently unfair." As a result, the survivor learns to "adopt a position of complete surrender," and develops an extraordinary ability to "scan for warning signs of attack," leaving the survivor with "fundamental problems in basic trust, autonomy, and initiative." By virtue of our age alone, our brain was less developed than the brain of our caregivers, and less developed than our brain as an adult.

In the present, in the now, we have more experience, we have more strength and resources, and we can influence the present to change it to our advantage. There was no hope of autonomy back then, but there is every hope of it now.

To reach beyond the confines of her relationship with Paul, and to achieve some sense of autonomy, Jackie had to break free of some of the imprisoning messages taught to her by her mother and stepfather. Slowly she started to realize that maybe, just maybe, her mother had been wrong to call her "good for nothing" as she gripped her bony fingers into Jackie's shoulders. (She would whisper this close to Jackie's ear, and Jackie could smell the rum and Coke on her breath.) Jackie could now see that her mother had been wrong because Jackie had a friend who was kind to her, and who told Jackie that she was "adorable." She also had a neighbor who told her that she was "easy to talk to, and funny."

As surely as her mother's message lost its grip on her, Jackie was no longer haunted by that smell of rum which had lingered around her mind for so long. She could breathe freely, and in that space to breathe, that space that looks like autonomy, she could see that it was wrong of her mother to tell her that she regretted ever giving birth to her. "You were a nasty baby," she would tell Jackie. "After the delight that was your sister, you came along and ruined everything. You never stopped screaming, and I swear that I was this close to throwing you off the balcony of the apartment." When Jackie had been a child, they lived on the fifth floor of an apartment block, and Jackie always wondered whether she would feel any pain if her mother ever acted on those words.

Even though the immediate concern when she entered therapy was Paul's use of coercion and control, Jackie's first step towards autonomy was to create a healthy distance from her abusive mother. Even in adulthood, she had continued to allow her mother to chip away at her self-esteem, always making excuses for her mother's cruel words and behavior. But suddenly one day, she turned around and told her mother that she was not going to have any contact with her until her mother found a more compassionate tone to use. For many who knew Jackie's mother, this seemed shocking as they only ever saw her as a kind, elderly lady. *Helpless and sweet.* Careful to keep things sealed off behind closed doors, making the family home a prison, Jackie's mother never let them see the brutality she had inflicted upon her daughter for all those years.

To reach beyond the confines of her childhood of abuse, it is important that Jackie is believed. Often survivors of trauma have trouble with telling their story because they fear people will judge them or not believe them. Too often perpetrators project an image of virtue to the outside world while they terrorize their children within the home. Cognitive dissonance means that we would rather ignore the suspected abuse than admit that we had it wrong about this smiling pillar of the community who sits on every committee of the PTA. Perpetrators will often switch the script so they are seen as the helpless victim and the adult survivor is the wrongdoer who has abandoned their helpless parent. The prison guard poses as the imprisoned.

**

Respite – Faulty messages from childhood

To act with autonomy, we need to view ourselves in the clear light of day, free of imprisoning messages from our past. Here are just some of the beliefs that we can end up developing because of these imprisoning messages:

- I am unworthy
- I am not good enough
- I am bad
- I am dirty
- I have no value
- I am shameful
- I am not trustworthy
- I cannot trust
- I am not safe
- I am powerless
- I am helpless
- I have no choice

**

If you have experienced trauma, including the type of adverse childhood experiences that Jackie grew up with, you can end up "continuing to organize your life as if the trauma were still going on—unchanged and immutable—as every new encounter or event is contaminated by the past," wrote van der Kolk in *The Body Keeps the Score*. When Jackie was a child enduring her mother's daily abuse, she depended on her mother for survival. Jackie learned quickly how to organize her life, so she could repress her own needs and feelings in favor of her mother's. As van der Kolk commented in "The Compulsion to Repeat the Trauma: Re-Enactment, Revictimization, and Masochism": "when the persons who are supposed to be the sources of safety and nurturance become simultaneously the sources of danger against which protection is needed, children maneuver to re-establish some sense of safety. Instead of turning on their caregivers and thereby losing hope for protection, they blame themselves. They become fearfully and hungrily attached and anxiously obedient." No matter how many years elapsed since she escaped her mother's home, still Jackie organized her life in a way that complied with Paul's instructions. She repressed her needs and feelings in favor of Paul's needs, remaining anxiously obedient to Paul no matter how much discomfort this might cause her.

However, no matter how long abuse contaminates your relationships, there is always the hope of a decontamination process with the help of nurturing, healthy relationships away from your abusers. This might start with an experienced trauma therapist or a compassionate friend or family member. One person I know found freedom and autonomy with the support of a friend he played golf with. No matter where you find this source of support, a healing part of the process is to tell your trauma story at a pace that feels safe and comfortable. It can be overwhelming to unpack a story of abuse, especially when it was at the hands of someone who should have kept you safe. It is too easy to blame yourself with questions such as "Am I really that unlovable for my own parent to have treated me that way?" By telling your trauma story to someone who respects your autonomy, you can discover that these experiences were not your fault.

The prison of a trauma bond

Trauma is hell on earth. Trauma resolved is a gift from the gods.

- Peter A. Levine

When I work with survivors of abuse, I can see it's hard for them to manage the dizzying contradiction that the person who is abusive can sometimes seem so charming, especially in front of other people. Yet close the door, turn your back, and reality comes crashing down around your ears. When we are young and the perpetrator is a caregiver, we depend on that person for our survival, and so we will do anything to be okay. We will accept any amount of torment to survive, and so we shut down our responses, falling into line with their orders out of fear of extinction. And when the sun shines, when they offer us a smile or a gentle touch rather than a slap, our heart can break open with relief. It is okay again; we are safe for a little longer. Quite the dizzying rollercoaster that is, as Herman describes, the "dialectic of trauma."

It was a mild August morning when Clark Olofsson and Jan-Erik Olsson seized control of Sveriges Kreditbanken, a bank in downtown Stockholm. Events were captured on live television, a rarity for 1970s Sweden, as four employees of the bank were captured and held for six days in a vault. Little did these hostages know that they would go down in history as the first to demonstrate what came to be known as *Stockholm syndrome*. Instead of fear or hatred for Olofsson and Olsson, the hostages developed an emotional attachment to their captors. A year later—this time across the Atlantic in the United States—heiress to the William Randolph Hearst newspaper company, Patricia Hearst, was kidnapped by the

Symbionese Liberation Army. This sounds like just another kidnapping until you learn that Hearst *helped* her captors to rob the Hibernia bank in California. The following decade, Terry Anderson, Terry Waite, and Thomas Sutherland were taken as hostages in Lebanon, and they later described how they were treated well by their captors, despite having been kept in solitary confinement under brutal conditions. It was as if they were covering up for their captors in a similar way that we hear survivors of domestic violence, attempting to minimize the abusive behavior they have endured.

Stockholm syndrome is not an official diagnosis, and the nature of hostage taking means that data tends to derive from autobiographies and biographies. As a result, there is no consistent definition or use of the phrase amongst professionals, but in general we can rely on the definition given by Namnyak et al in "'Stockholm Syndrome': Psychiatric Diagnosis Or Urban Myth?": Each captee "experienced direct threats, they were kept in isolation, had an opportunity to escape during their period of captivity but failed to use it and showed sympathy with their captors post captivity." To apply Polyvagal Theory, you could argue that the captees showed signs of the *fawn* response. As mentioned earlier in this book, this has been defined by psychotherapist Peter Walker in "Codependency, Trauma and the Fawn Response" as "servitude, ingratiation, and forfeiture of any needs that might inconvenience and ire" the aggressor. The fawn response is a survival strategy, and, faced with armed aggressors, you can see how it might have kept the captees alive.

In "The Compulsion to Repeat the Trauma: Re-Enactment, Revictimization, and Masochism" van der Kolk explains that we are "strongly dependent on social support for a sense of safety, meaning, power, and control." In the face of danger, we seek attachment or, in other words, "pain, fear, fatigue, and loss of loved ones and protectors all evoke efforts to attract increased care." Furthermore, "when there is no access to ordinary sources of comfort, people may turn toward their tormentors." And here, we are not just referring to hostages. In abusive domestic relationships, a process of traumatic bonding between abuser and survivor has been observed. As van der Kolk explains, violence can create confusion that interferes with our memory, "and this memory only returns fully during renewed terror." It can be hard to break a traumatic bond that leaves you feeling dizzy with the contradiction that the person can be kind and loving at one moment, and terrifying the next. This can explain why it is so hard to reach beyond the confines of coercion and control and realize our autonomy. It is why it took so many years for Jackie to see what was happening with her mother, and then with Paul. How difficult it can be to reach for autonomy when we are caught in a cycle of punishment and reward, arousal, and peace.

Difficult, but not impossible.

**

Respite – Features of the trauma bond

A trauma bond is not an official diagnostic term, but it has been used to describe the process in abusive relationships of all kinds. Here is what a trauma bond looks like:

- One person (the captor) exercises undue coercion or control over the other (the captee). For example, the captor uses intimidation and threats or the use of violence
- The captor keeps the captee on the receiving end of a cycle of manipulation and kindness
- The captor tries to keep the captee isolated from others
- The captee feels dependent on the captor
- Despite the coercive treatment, the captee describes positive feelings towards the captor
- The captee will often minimize the captor's behavior

**

Autonomy does not equate to isolation

If a tree falls in a forest and no one is around to hear it, does it make a sound?

- George Berkeley

Should Jackie leave Paul, she might resolve to spend the rest of her life alone. After all the pain of coercion, isolation might seem like just the analgesic that she needs. But autonomy does not have to equate to isolation, which Xavier did not yet appreciate when he said, "I don't need anyone in my life, I can go it alone."

Twenty-five-year-old Xavier had been crushed by an endless stream of relationships that self-destructed, and he was determined to give up on the whole idea of connection. He was aware of the benefits to his physical and mental health, and he appreciated the Polyvagal Theory of the autonomic nervous system, placing the *social engagement system* at the optimum level, but he was simply unwilling to expose himself to the risk of yet more heartache.

What Xavier did not appreciate was that autonomy can never be absolute. We experience it or strive for it, but there is never a time when we are completely free. In our early years, when we are dependent on our caregivers for survival, we have a very low degree of autonomy. As the years go by, our autonomy should increase as we learn and grow. But even in adulthood, under the most ideal conditions, we have some sense of restriction or accountability to others, whether in the form of a formal penal code or in less-formal social sanctions. Avoiding other people is extremely hard, so we must compromise our absolute autonomy, through cooperation and empathy, to survive. We may not need to go out hunting in packs anymore, but we do need to earn a living, and that usually involves other people. We need to meet our medical needs, and that involves other people. And we need each other to continue developing our brains in terms of self-awareness. Knowledge of yourself is incomplete unless you understand yourself in relationship with other people. Without this level of self-awareness, we remain imprisoned by our thoughts and emotions, or, in the words of John A. Johnson, PhD, our "*unconscious scripts*."

These scripts remain unconscious until we become aware of our process. And the more aware we are, the greater autonomy we can enjoy. In the words of psychiatrist Eric Berne in *Games People Play*, "awareness requires living in the here and now, and not in the elsewhere, the past or the future… The aware person is alive because he knows how he feels, where he is and when it is." Awareness of your process involves a conscious effort to continuously monitor your thought patterns, the way you regulate your emotions, and your behavior.

Taking this a little further: How does the external environment impact you? For example, you might notice that you feel anxious around certain types of people or in certain situations. Around other people you might feel drained of energy or detached from your emotions. One person might feel suffocated around someone who talks a lot, whereas someone else might feel this way around someone who is uncommunicative. The point is to try and carve out time and space to slowly start to recognize patterns so you can gain a better sense of your process. And with greater insight, you have a better chance of autonomy. This can be hard to do in the rush and hustle of everyday life, and your process fires away at lightning speed every day. Unless we take the time to stop and reflect on our process, we can end up becoming hijacked by certain events, people, or internal states. We can make short-circuited conclusions about what changes we need to make in our life.

The more we are aware of our process—whether our general thought patterns, emotional patterns, or patterns of behavior—the more autonomy we can enjoy. With awareness we choose how to respond rather than responding like an automaton controlled by unconscious assumptions and impulses. We become less vulnerable to our *unconscious scripts*.

To help them gain awareness of their process, I often suggest that clients keep a simple "trigger log" for whenever something makes them feel strongly, whether the feeling is anxious, depressed, fearful, angry, or any other strong emotion. In *Beyond the Blue* I detailed what this log entails (I refer to it as the *ABC log*), and how to use it. But whether you use a structured trigger log or a simple journal of your thoughts, emotions, and behaviors, many therapists like me, believe that writing things out can help you to identify patterns, organize your thoughts, and gain acceptance of your internal state. The process of writing can also serve as a moment of catharsis, giving you a sense of distance from your distress.

Twenty-seven-year-old Katia was buzzing with energy when she first started therapy. She would rush into the session ten or fifteen minutes late, caught up in a flurry of distractions about her journey to the appointment, or an argument with her boyfriend, or a success in her business, which was starting to take off. It was easy to get carried away with Katia's freneticism because she painted such vivid stories with intricate descriptions of every surrounding fact. And throughout this vivid storytelling she smiled and laughed heartily, portraying the image of someone who was full of life. But it was all an act. Katia was in agony inside, devastated by the loss of her brother, who had been killed in a skiing accident the previous year. She was lurching from one distraction to the next, working late into the night, drinking too much with friends, and watching endless television while she ate with a blank stare. She knew something had to change, but she did not know where to begin.

To realize her autonomy, Katia had to gain awareness of how she was distracting herself from her brother's death, and how she was operating on autopilot. She had to understand that her initial way of coping with her brother's death, through overworking, excessive drinking, and overeating, might have helped her with the initial shock of the news, but these are not sustainable coping strategies. They do not foster a true sense of freedom from within.

In *Full Catastrophe Living*, Kaban-Zinn claims that mindfulness is the best way to achieve the level of awareness necessary to realize true autonomy. Although they agree that mindfulness is helpful, professor Kirk Warren Brown and Richard M. Ryan claim that mindfulness offers more than just *awareness*. In "The Benefits of Being Present: Mindfulness and its Role in Psychological Well-Being," Brown and Ryan explain that mindfulness helps you to achieve *consciousness*. "Consciousness encompasses both awareness and attention," write Brown and Ryan, because "awareness is the background 'radar' of consciousness, continually monitoring the inner and outer environment. One may be aware of stimuli without them being at the center of attention. Attention is a process of focusing conscious awareness, providing heightened sensitivity to a limited range of experience (Westen, 1999). In actuality, awareness and attention are intertwined, such that attention continually pulls 'figures' out of the 'ground' of awareness, holding them focally for varying lengths of time."

Brown and Ryan explain that mindfulness can help us enhance our "attention to and awareness of current experience or present reality" instead of becoming "blunted or restricted." Slowly, Katia began to see how her life had become blunted by overworking, excessive drinking, and overeating, and as she engaged more with the present, she started to make more informed choices about what she consumed, and how much she worked. It was early in her work, and there were many other parts to her therapeutic journey, but it was a start.

An over-correction in search of autonomy

One of the foundational principles of the American Counseling Association's code of ethics is autonomy, or "fostering the right to control the direction of one's life." However, this must be weighed against the other foundational principles of non-maleficence (a duty to avoid harm), beneficence (an obligation to work for the good of the client and society), justice (treating clients fairly), fidelity (being trustworthy), and veracity (telling the truth). This means that even if a client wished to exercise their autonomy and end their life, a therapist could not stand by without alerting the authorities. The principle of non-maleficence requires a therapist to ensure the safety of this person. This makes sense because depression, which can often contribute to suicidal intent, causes cognitive constriction, which means a person does not think clearly when they are depressed. In other words, someone who is suicidal might not otherwise wish to exercise the autonomy of suicide if not for the cognitive constriction caused by the depression. As psychologist Kenneth France points out in his book *Crisis Intervention*: "Many suicidal persons display cognitive restriction. And their rigid thinking often leads to difficulties in identifying problems and potential solutions, as demonstrated in empirical research."

Leila slammed her hand in the door as she joined the session with her new therapist. She was suspicious of new settings and, given the choice, she preferred to run the risk of offending someone than get "screwed over." And Leila had every reason not to trust. When she was just ten years old her mother sent her to the US from Mexico, where she would stay with an aunt who quickly grew tired of her presence. Her aunt's boyfriend, on the other hand, took an unhealthy interest in her, and so she spent most of her childhood either outside of the home, or, if she could not avoid being at home, making sure her door was wedged shut with a chest of drawers. On occasion, her aunt's boyfriend would come home drunk, and if he could not get into Leila's room, he would take out his frustrations by beating Leila's aunt with his belt.

One night, when she was fourteen, Leila could hear her aunt's boyfriend trying to get in the front door. At first she thought it was the wind, which had been whipping about the house, slamming the shutters against the window. When she realized it was her aunt's boyfriend hammering at the door, she raced down the stairs.

As soon as she heard the solid thud of bolt unlocking, she realized she had made a mistake. Years later, each time she recounted this story, she berated herself for opening the front door. "Why did I do it? I am so stupid. I could have left him out in the rain, and he would have had to find some other place to take shelter."

The door slammed against the wall with the sound of shattering glass. When Leila saw his drenched clothes and glaring eyes, she knew she had a split second to find safety before he would be whipping his belt out to punish her. She raced up the stairs and slammed her bedroom door behind her, wedging the chest of drawers against it to give herself time to think about her next move. She knew she had seen a flash of color as she climbed the stairs, and she knew that was her aunt appearing from the kitchen. And she knew that her aunt would be her boyfriend's target, now Leila was out of range. Even today, she can hear the screams from her aunt, and she can still imagine the raw feeling as leather met skin at a ferocious rate. She heard her aunt pleading for mercy and the boyfriend threatening to kill her, so Leila dialed 911.

By the time the police came, her aunt needed stitches, but she was alive. From that moment there was a shift inside her, and Leila was determined to never feel that helplessness again. She would ferociously protect her autonomy no matter what. The trouble was, years later, she had overcorrected that sense of helplessness that overwhelmed her that night. She was seeing dangers in darkened corners that might have held hope, and her friends were retreating from her, all tired of her mistrust. She was so determined to protect her autonomy that she was imprisoning herself in a life of isolation. We need to feel safe, but we also need to feel love. We must protect our autonomy, but not at any cost.

Is autonomy an illusion?

To see a World in a Grain of Sand
And a heaven in a Wild Flower,
Hold Infinity in the palm of your hand
And Eternity in an hour.
- William Blake

If we are to reach beyond our confines and strive for autonomy, a freedom from undue external control or coercion, this suggests that we need to know where the dividing line is between freedom and confinement. The trouble is, the parameters of autonomy are not clearly demarcated like the boundary of four prison walls. It isn't easy to identify when we are influenced by the imprisoning messages we carry around from our past, for example. And our thought patterns, methods of emotion regulation, and behavior might have resulted from the influence of others. Autonomy seems even more illusory when we consider how the environment in which we live (natural and man-made) is influenced by, and influences, us. Every moment we create meaning for our environment and the people in it, so we, in a way, pollute the very autonomy that we think that we are striving for.

The concept of pure autonomy has been criticized by feminist theorists "for failing to take into account situated and relational social determinants of the individual that cause and/or constitute and/or compromise autonomy in decision-making," wrote Jonathan Beever and Nicolae Morar in "The Porosity of Autonomy."

Biologists also criticize the concept of pure autonomy, preferring instead to identify a process of *interaction* when they explain the relationship of the environment and what lives within it. For example, as A. Grandpierre and Menas Kafatos explain in "Biological Autonomy," "cells act on microscopic, quantum states, e.g., initiate spontaneous emissions and couple them to spontaneous absorptions useful for biological aims." In other words, "parts and wholes cannot exist independently of each other, and the whole serves as the ground for the existence of the parts."

What all of this suggests is that freedom is not just about the identification of a clear dividing line between our autonomy and confinement. That does not always exist. In fact, freedom is not just about freedom to make choices without the coercion or control of others. After all, if we are to reach beyond our confines, we need to know the answer to these questions:

What is too much or too little freedom?

Does the measure of freedom that we currently enjoy give us a life that reflects the values we have chosen as part of our self-identity?

To use autonomy to answer these would only give us half the picture. After all, we can live a life that we have chosen, without the coercion or control of others, but still end up miserable. It is safe to say, therefore, that when it comes to the key to free your mind, autonomy is necessary, but it is not sufficient. To answer the questions set out above, to reach beyond your confines and truly free your mind, you need something more than autonomy that is rationally verified. You need to know that you are living *authentically.*

How can we identify this further step beyond our confines, a life authentically verified?

CHAPTER 9

The personal resonance of authenticity

Only the truth of who you are, if realized, will set you free.
- Eckhart Tolle

Mark lived free of the dictates of others. He prided himself on his autonomy, living free of the coercion or control of others, and he isolated himself to such an extent that he referred to his home as a fortress. He dismissed friends and family members as "a distraction," and he prided himself on his ability to focus on his career as a senior attorney in Chicago. He had developed a razor-sharp focus, dismissing others without even glancing up from his work, and if they did not take the hint, he would shut the door of his office so he could continue uninterrupted. It was not a life of comfort, and he allowed no room for spontaneity, flexibility, or any other characteristic that paint the multicolored images that define human nature.

It was inevitable that Mark would eventually feel the discomfort of this unnatural existence. Even if he was not immediately aware of it, the frustrations of his own making were starting to break out across his brow in the form of stress-infused beads of sweat. He started to snap and snarl at everyone's mistakes, including his own, and eventually his colleagues began avoiding him altogether, which is when the senior partner at his firm took notice.

"Things have to change," Mark was told, after the senior partner took a turn shutting Mark's office door. He did not smile or attempt to soften the message in any way. His direct delivery was half the reason he had so quickly risen to such a senior position in the firm.

"You need to make changes now," he said. "You cannot treat other people as if they are objects. Shape up, Mark, or you're out. And if you can't find a way to change, good luck finding any other place to work. I can't think of many careers that don't require the art of collaboration."

Before joining the law firm in Chicago, Mark had grown up in West Virginia without ever knowing his father. His mother often changed jobs, and they moved frequently to avoid debt collectors or her latest ex-boyfriend, forcing Mark to constantly adapt to new schools. He craved stability, and yet this was the one thing he lacked, as he constantly bent himself out of shape, trying to fit in to cliques formed years before he arrived. Occasionally some kind person would invite him to their house, but this only made things worse, when he saw what little his own home life had to offer. He could not remember the last time he had sat at a table and eaten a meal with his mother. She left him to scavenge what he could from the refrigerator. He was never sure where she was, but her return home was often fraught with tension. He could not stand the heavy tang of whatever alcohol cast a cloud over her return, making her irritable and distant. Sometimes he wondered whether she even noticed that he was there, and so he learned to quiet himself, like a mouse, as she stumbled around the house until she found her bed. He sat in the shadows of her awareness, savoring memories of other people's houses, where the air was clear of alcohol, and there was food on the kitchen table, and the parents were present, talking about landscapers or work meetings or tennis tournaments. While Mark's mother stumbled in the dark—and it was unclear whether she was just unsure of her footing or her place in relationship to him (perhaps both)—other families seemed to understand their place, and the individuals their role in the family. People followed rituals, whether it was collecting the mail from the box outside or placing dirty plates in the dishwasher. There was a rhythm and a sense of certainty that resonated with him, and it was those qualities that made a home out of just a house.

But Mark felt like a misfit, and he had no part to play in this rhythm, so he became determined to create his own corner of the world, away from the imprisoning chaos of his mother's alcoholism. And so he created the fortress, and he spent years focusing his attention and defending that sense of autonomy from the coercion or control of any other person. The trouble was that he was lost within his own fortress. As the senior partner had pointed out, he would be hard-pressed to find a career that did not rely, at least in part, on collaboration. To live a life from within a fortress might show that he was living autonomously, that he was free of the coercion or control of others, but it was hardly freedom. He was miserable, and he was limiting his potential, something people with anxiety often do in an effort to remain safe from the things they fear.

The trouble is, safety is not our only need. We have a broad spectrum of needs, and when our needs are not met, our emotions tell us that things need to change. The beads of perspiration and incessant frustration were telling Mark that autonomy was not enough. He needed something more, something that personally resonated with him. Something that made him feel truly free.

The personal resonance of authenticity

If we are to reach beyond our confines, we need to know what we are reaching for. Although authenticity and autonomy are occasionally used synonymously, they are not the same. Autonomy requires a life to be self-governing as a result of a *rational reflective endorsement* of those choices. It is arguable that Mark has a life of autonomy. From a *rational* perspective, Mark can justify the safety and predictability of his own rituals inside the fortress of his own creation. He only has his career to worry about— no alcoholic who might come home late at night and do goodness knows what. Safe and predictable. But

Mark knows that something is missing. He *feels* this in his body. If autonomy is the foundation and structure of a house, authenticity is the fitting out, the furnishings, and the general ambience of a home. To live *authentically*, Mark has to use his *whole* being, not just his rational mind, to assess his life. To carry out this assessment, Mark must use his emotions and his body to get a *felt sense* of his life. Only then can he get a sense of whether he is living *authentically*, not just autonomously. He can ask himself whether there is a *personal resonance* to his life that reflects his values and beliefs. Is this life within the fortress really who he is, who he is supposed to be? Does this reflect the values he has chosen as part of his self-identity?

Kabat-Zinn points out that the meaning of *sapiens* in *homo sapiens* is "the present participle—indicating unfolding in the present moment—of the Latin verb *sapere*, to know, to taste, to perceive, to be wise. We are the knowing species. We are the species that has the capacity to know and to know that we know." This is a message of hope. It tells us that we have great wisdom within us, if we could just free our minds of the external distractions of life. In *The Power of Now*, Eckhart Tolle introduces a similar concept, but instead he uses "enlightenment" or "your natural state of felt oneness with Being," which, Tolle claims, can be achieved by living in the now. If only we could all slow down—stop, even—and recognize that enlightenment from within, we might discover the key to free our minds. Mark has the capacity to know that the fortress is not a life of authenticity. Given time and space, he will be able to sense this, to understand this. He just needs to stop for a moment and give himself time and space to discover the personal resonance of authenticity. This is something we all need to do on a regular basis if we are ever to reach beyond our confines.

Living in the now - The varying concepts of authenticity

Research shows that mindfulness is closely related to authenticity because of the importance, in both cases, of self-actualization. "Mindfulness," says Kabat-Zinn, helps with "authentic functioning— i.e., being aware of and regulating oneself," and research also shows that "cultivating a mindful or meditative attitude toward oneself and others" can result in significant benefits to physical and mental health. Given the benefits of mindfulness, and the significant overlap between mindfulness and authenticity, it is arguable that authenticity can produce a similarly beneficial result. According to Kabat-Zinn, the Buddha and many others who are deeply involved with mindfulness teach that there is suffering "that we make for ourselves on top of the suffering that comes from natural and human events that are beyond our ability to control." There is no avoiding the suffering from events beyond our control, but the additional suffering we make for ourselves on top of this is *unnecessary suffering*. "Pain may be inevitable, the suffering that accompanies it is optional," Kabat-Zinn writes in *Mindfulness for Beginners*.

Many therapists refer to authenticity, or a concept very similar to it, to distinguish a *true self* from a *false self.* According to Carl Jung, "one does not become enlightened by imagining figures of light, but by making the darkness conscious." Fritz Perls, the father of Gestalt therapy, refers to inauthenticity as "game-playing" and "an attempt to get away from oneself" or "neurosis." Existential therapists do not view authenticity as a true self but rather "an authentic way of Being-in-the-world," as explained in *Existential Therapy and Psychotherapeutic Practice*. For me, this gets a great deal closer to the concept of authenticity that I understand. The true self is a process that is always being discovered, and that process of discovery takes into account the environment within which we live. In the words of existential therapist Emmy van Deurzen in *Everyday Mysteries: Existential Dimensions of Psychotherapy*: ". . .my self is not a substantial entity. My I is like an eye, an iris, an opening which lets through the light of existence. Its function is to be transparent and to be open so that life (being) can shine through."

Discovery of an authentic way of being in the world often involves a painful confrontation of our truths about our existence. For example, we need to confront our mortality, isolation, freedom, and meaninglessness, and all of this can create anxiety. Our anxiety is compounded when we try to resist all of this, and so, in *A Year to Live*, Stephen Levine encourages us to “confront our life and death with mercy and awareness.” Levine suggests that we try to “live as consciously as possible,” and this is only possible if we “let go” and “trust the process.” Given our need to control and our need to manage our intolerance of uncertainty by seeking out more and more knowledge, even if that means we rely on the half-baked knowledge of others, this is admittedly a big ask. But it is not impossible.

Arguably, breaking free of our confines and reaching for authenticity means “learning to stay present even under difficult circumstances, to embrace mental, physical, and spiritual pain using techniques suitable for each particular level of discomfort,” Levine writes. According to Levine, if we prepare for our death, boundaries are lifted so that “previous hindrances to joy and mercy toward self and others melt into an increasingly expanding awareness and appreciation of the present.” When I have worked with people facing their own mortality, their pain has increased when they have denied or fought the news. Only when they finally accept the reality, and they accept the pain that comes with it, do I notice a softening in their demeanor. As Rumi put it: “The wound is the place where the Light enters you.”

Somatic resonance

There is deep wisdom within our very flesh, if we can only come to our senses and feel it.

- Elizabeth Behnke

Somatic means “of the body.” You can use your body to register experiences or memories, and you can also use your body to identify a *personal resonance of authenticity*. You feel the ground under your feet when you walk through a park, and so you can also sense an emotion in your body. You feel the warmth of joy spreading through your belly, or the fizz of fear in your chest. This is sensing the personal resonance of authenticity in your body.

Many types of therapists focus on the body as part of their work. Somatic therapists direct the client to become more aware of their body, and the therapist can also use their own body to gain a deeper insight into what might be going on for their client. Peter Levine developed an approach to therapy called *Somatic Experiencing* that emphasizes awareness of the body to heal from trauma and resolve other mental health challenges. For example, you may not immediately recognize the fear, but you have a felt sense, somewhere in your body, of it. One systematic approach to the use of the body to identify deeper insight is *focusing*, an approach introduced by philosopher Eugene Gendlin. Gendlin encourages you to clear a space in your body and mind so you can get a "felt sense" within your body of the problem. It is helpful to ask yourself "What is the main thing for me right now?" Then identify a word or image that comes up from that felt sense," and check to see if that word or image resonates with the felt sense. Once you have a word or image that resonates with the felt sense, ask yourself "What is it, about this whole problem that makes this quality?" Continue checking in with your body to see if this answer resonates with your body.

When I first held my daughter, the moment she was born, my arms became solid blocks of ice. I was frozen with fear that such a beautiful, fragile human being could be in my arms. If I had found this crippling and was unable to function as a parent, Gendlin would have encouraged me to clear my mind and go into the center of my felt sense of this frozen feeling. This deeper awareness might have led to a clearer sense of what I was telling myself to create this fear (for example "I am going to fail," or "Mistakes are unacceptable"). This might have helped to clear the way for me to identify what I needed, including support from other people, or reassurance of the things I was doing right.

It is now recognized that we can know things beyond our thoughts, and we can sense things using more than our five senses. In *Mindfulness for Beginners*, Kabat-Zinn offers the example of knowing where you are right now, without thinking about it. This sense of knowing orients you in time and space. Kabat-Zinn refers to the concept of proprioception or "the sense of knowing and feeling the body's position in space both statically and in motion." The concept of interoception is "the sense of knowing how your body is feeling from the inside. It is not based on thinking about how your body is, but on the direct experiencing of it. It is an internal, embodied, *feeling*, a felt sense," Kabat-Zinn explains. Just as societies such as the United States favor extroversion, we have become a species who also favor wisdom that is mined from external sources. We are quite inventive beings, but those inventions tend to take us further and further away from our inner core. We google a question before we have stopped to think about whether we already know the answer; we seek verification and validation and reassurance from others who we know less about than ourselves; and we pay more than we can afford to lean on experts who tell us what we already know. Yet we have so much knowledge that already exists within us and just need time and space to discover that wisdom, which takes a resetting of the balance between our internal and external sources of information. From there, we might be able to reach beyond our confines, using both wisdom from without and from within.

The great resignation – a wave of authenticity?

If Mark had ever been able to listen to anyone beyond his senior partner, if he had let just one friend or family member into his life, he might have been encouraged to follow the trend set by millions of other people in the US. Someone might have convinced him that he could only reach beyond his confines and realize a personal resonance of authenticity if he quit his job and made a fresh start.

"The Great Resignation" is a phrase coined by Texas A&M professor of business administration Anthony Klotz to explain the resignation of 4.3 million workers in the US in August 2021. According to the "Jobs Openings and Labor Turnover Summary," a report published by the US Bureau of Labor Statistics, this represented the highest number of quits since December 2000. Klotz points out that in the US, who we are in our jobs is central to our identity, and he suggests that the pandemic might have raised even more than the usual existential questions about life and happiness. In this pandemic, many might have asked themselves whether their work life reflected who they were. Based on this line of reasoning, you can see how some might argue that the Great Resignation was an act of authenticity on a mass scale. Suddenly millions of people in the US were reaching beyond the confines of jobs they no longer enjoyed and were possibly striving for that personal resonance of authenticity.

There are many reasons why someone might resign from a job, so to refer to everyone's decision as a sign of authenticity might be misguided. We cannot be sure that in every case their resignation reflected a sense of self-identity. For example, someone might have resigned to escape an abusive boss, or they might have been forced out by a malicious coworker. However, 4.3 million resignations is a huge number so we cannot ignore it, especially when it coincided with such a game-changing event as a pandemic. The pandemic challenged so much of what we once took for granted, so it will be interesting to see how this trend develops, and what relationship this has with authenticity.

Authenticity is an ongoing process

Mark did not have one conversation with his senior partner and then magically discover a more authentic life. In *Kierkegaard's Philosophy: Self-Deception and Cowardice in the Present Age*, John Mullen describes authenticity as "ongoing acts of courage." As new challenges arose over the years, Mark continued to evaluate what he endorsed from a rational perspective. Now, however, he knew that his decisions also had to reflect his self-identity. This self-identity was still taking shape over time, but he could feel, as a matter of personal resonance throughout his body, that this identity existed beyond the four walls of his fortress.

We can see now that neither authenticity nor autonomy are a fixed place or a destination. We are continuously in flux, and so we need ongoing acts of courage to strive for autonomy that is rationally endorsed as well as ongoing acts of courage that give us that personal resonance of authenticity, a life that reflects our self-identity. This continual process is interconnected with the environment in which we live. Our freedom is realized and limited in relationship with other people and other things. Reaching beyond your confines to escape an Internal Prison of your own creation is not just an exercise in individual growth, it also inevitably influences, and is influenced by the External Prison of structural inequality and privilege.

How do we reach beyond the confines of an External Prison of structural inequality and privilege?

CHAPTER 10

Beyond the confines of structural inequality and privilege

So distribution should undo excess,
And each man have enough.
- William Shakespeare

...bars can't build better men and misery can only break what goodness remains
- Stuart Turton

-

The 1800s saw a cholera epidemic sweep through America. According to Elizabeth Fenn of University of Colorado Boulder, the white protestants mostly blamed the outbreaks on the Irish immigrants, –a common theme in pandemics. After all, if we look to the next century, we find the 1918 pandemic, which some called the "Spanish flu" even though it likely originated at a military base in Fort Riley, Kansas. Fast forward to the 1950s and the polio outbreaks were blamed on Black Americans and poor people. And many of us can still remember the toxic messages that were communicated in the 1980s when the LGBTQ+ community was blamed for HIV-AIDS. There are echoes of that even now, with the current 2022 monkeypox outbreak. In 2020, after some news outlets referred to COVID-19 as the "Wuhan virus" or the "China virus," there was a disturbing rise in attacks on Asian Americans and Pacific Islanders. I remember some of my own friends reporting how scared they felt just walking the streets alone. No matter how much we reach beyond the confines of our Internal Prison, structural inequality—including racism, sexism, capitalism, heteronormativity, and ableism, to name a handful—is the hardest prison to break out of. Do all you can to escape the Internal Prison of your thought process, your emotional dysregulation, and even the imprisoning messages given to you during an abusive childhood, and there is still an External Prison just waiting to confine you like a nightmare that you keep trying to wake up from.

Structural inequality is "an inequality in the distribution of a valued resource, such as wealth, information, or technology, that brings social power." According to Dayna Bowen Matthew, Dean and Harold H. Greene professor of law at the George Washington University Law School, structural inequality "delivers cumulative advantage to the affluent—and cumulative disadvantage to others—by disparately allocating access to education, employment, housing, food, healthcare, political power, and legal representation." Further, "Structural inequality is directly associated with poor health in the United States and globally," including mental health, and it is seen as "the greatest threat to our health as a society," as explained in "Structural Inequality: The Real COVID-19 Threat to America's Health and How Strengthening the Affordable Care Act Can Help."

The COVID-19 pandemic did not create structural inequality and privilege, but it certainly exacerbated the problems that arise from it. As Matthew points out, "The pandemic demonstrated that structural racism threatens the health and well-being of the entire American population and economy." The pandemic did not hit all communities equally. According to the Kaiser Family Foundation (KFF), a nonprofit organization focusing on national health issues, "the pandemic has disproportionately affected the health of communities of color" because "non-Hispanic Black adults (48%) and Hispanic or Latino adults (46%) are more likely to report symptoms of anxiety and/or depressive disorder than Non-Hispanic White adults (41%)." In addition, "compared to nonessential workers, essential workers are more likely to report symptoms of anxiety or depressive disorder (42% vs. 30%), starting or increasing substance use (25% vs. 11%), and suicidal thoughts (22% vs. 8%) during the pandemic."

To reach beyond the confines of our Internal Prison, to achieve a true sense of autonomy or authenticity, we need to reach the daylight of awareness. It is difficult to maintain good mental health when we are trapped within ignorance, so we need to open our eyes to the part we play in structural inequality. Whether we benefit from it or are burdened by it, we need to see it for what it is. Without awareness of our privilege and structural inequality, we perpetuate the oppression that keeps us all trapped within an unhealthy society. For example, I must acknowledge my own privilege as someone who is white, who was given the male label at birth, who is college educated, and who is a mental health professional. I am part of this structural inequality, and so I need to remain vigilant to how my privilege might harm others. As we can see from the devastation of environmental pollution, there is no clear dividing line between *them* and *us*. We are all interrelated, and so we are all affected by and affect each other. Our Internal and External Prisons continuously affect each other, and so awareness of one ultimately involves, and impacts, the other. And just as we can construct these prisons to confine us, so we can also discover the keys to escape them.

Intersectional theory offers one key to a better understanding of structural inequality and privilege. According to sociologist Taylor W. Hargrove, of Carolina Population Center at the University of North Carolina at Chapel Hill, looking at one factor, such as racism or sexism, is not enough. We need to examine the intersection of different social statuses, including race, gender, and class. For example, as outlined in "Structural Racism and Inequalities in Health," one study revealed that "Black and Asian American women consistently reported the highest levels of depressive symptoms throughout adolescence and young adulthood" and these disadvantages "may have been overlooked in studies examining either race or gender disparities." When it comes to structural inequality, it is not enough to understand one factor, such as race or gender. We need to understand how these factors *intersect*.

We only need to turn on the news today to see how intersectional theory can illustrate how structural inequality and privilege still creates the ultimate prison. This year the United States Supreme Court has decided to overturn Roe v Wade, a 1973 Supreme Court decision that once recognized a woman's right to abortion as protected by the Constitution. Some argue that this poses a threat to women across the United States, but, according to Jamila Taylor, director of health care reform at The Century Foundation, the reality is that this decision will mainly impact low-income women of color. Just as we saw that the pandemic hit certain communities more than others, this level of detail can only be appreciated with the aid of intersectional theory. It also helps us to see who made this damaging decision: a group of mainly Roman Catholic, straight, white, cisgender men.

Intersectional theory can help us understand the subtleties of the trauma of discrimination, privilege, and structural inequality. The phrase *intersectionality* was first coined in 1989 by Kimberlé Crenshaw of UCLA School of Law and Columbia Law School, and since then, in the words of Anne Sisson Runyan, professor of public and international affairs at University of Cincinnati, the concept has been developed to "counter unidimensional and exclusionary analyses of oppression in many disciplines." One example Runyan offers is "the reduction of feminist inquiry to examining only the experiences of white, Western women." Runyan points out that intersectional theory offers an understanding of how we comprise various "albeit constructed and provisional" identities that are "based on race, true gender identity, class, nationality, sexuality, physical (dis)ability, religion, and age," and intersectional theory helps us to understand how the intersection of these identities "confer various disadvantages and privileges on each of us." Whether you are the beneficiary (and therefore the oppressor) or the victim of privilege and structural inequality, intersectional theory can help us to reach beyond the confines of that oppression. As Runyan explains in "What Is Intersectionality and Why Is It Important," intersectional theory disrupts "hierarchies of oppression based, for example, on claims that class oppression trumps all other forms of oppression or that gender oppression is the originary oppression or that racial oppression must be primary to the exclusion of others."

A WEIRD color-blind eye?

Another one of the foundational principles of the American Counseling Association's code of ethics is beneficence. This is an obligation to work for the good of the client *and society*, and yet some therapists believe that their job description begins and ends with the individual client. The pandemic really highlighted the need to address structural reform, and yet some healthcare professionals (usually who are white, cisgender, and straight) still claim no contradiction with this ethical principle and their support of a certain former president, police brutality, or countless other institutions that incite and perpetuate the trauma that their clients are trying to survive. Clearly there is a conflict of interests, no less than healthcare professionals who assault their clients with microaggressions such as "I don't see color," "I don't mind if you are gay, it is irrelevant to our work," or misgendering or deadnaming their clients.

We also have a duty to acknowledge the lack of representation amongst mental health research (and health research generally). As mental health practitioners, we are required to use evidence-based interventions, and yet there is widespread acknowledgement that the evidence upon which many of these interventions are based is far from representative. As Joseph Henrich, professor of human evolutionary biology, writes in "The Weirdest People in the World?," "Behavioral scientists routinely publish broad claims about human psychology." However, the samples that these scientists use are entirely derived from "Western, Educated, Industrialized, Rich and Democratic (WEIRD) societies." Henrich adds that members of these societies are "the least representative populations one could find for generalizing about humans." As a result, Henrich urges us to become "less cavalier in addressing questions of human nature on the basis of data drawn from this particularly thin, and rather unusual, slice of humanity."

When I am challenged about my work as a social justice advocate and how I reconcile this with my career as a psychotherapist, I point to Kabat-Zinn who was brutalized by the police in the 1970s as he protested the Vietnam war. Then a student at Massachusetts Institute of Technology, I can imagine how Kabat-Zinn might have reconciled this protest as an attempt to stop the creation of more trauma, explaining that his resistance to the police was required of him, not an act of contradiction or inappropriate. Jump ahead to more recent years, and Kabat-Zinn, in "Too Early to Tell: The Potential Impact and Challenges—Ethical and Otherwise—Inherent in the Mainstreaming of Dharma in an Increasingly Dystopian World," now blames "the ascendency of Trump and the forces and values he represents" for so much suffering that is being caused in the world. He explains that there is a "growing mindset of populism around the globe" and this is creating more racism, police violence, and "fear and mistreatment of immigrants." Kabat-Zinn urges us to address structural issues such as "social and economic injustices in our inner cities, the energy and pipeline wars pitting the power of the state against indigenous people on their own land," and "the growing concerns about the accessibly of clean water." Without addressing all of this, we cannot have mental health any more than we can grow an orchid without oxygen or water. Because we are all interconnected, mental health is not just about an individual's health, something that was implied by Enrique Salmón in "Kincentric Ecology: Indigenous Perceptions of the Human Nature Relationship." As mentioned earlier in this book, Salmón introduced the concept of *kincentricity* to explain that we are all "part of an extended ecological family," and "life in any environment is viable only when humans view the life surrounding them as kin. The kin, or relatives, include all the natural elements of an ecosystem," and so we all "are affected by and, in turn, affect the life around" us. Salmón adds that the "interactions that result from this '*kincentric ecology*' enhance and preserve the ecosystem," and, in parallel, I would add that we are all affected by—and, in turn, affect—structural inequality. Without recognition of our role in this inequality, we all suffer, and if we take steps to break down the walls of this External Prison, we will all benefit.

Compassion and unity

If we are to break down the walls of the prison of structural inequality and privilege, we need to see the commonality amongst us, and to do this, we need to develop a sense of compassion. As National Youth Poet Laureate Amanda Gorman put it in *Call Us What We Carry*, "Lost as we feel, there is no better / Compass than compassion." If we all have a compass of compassion, why do some of us use it less than others? Compassion is awareness of another person's suffering, and a wish for that suffering to end. The origin of the word means *to suffer together*, and through this lens we can see that we are all human, and so we are all capable of making mistakes. Compassion helps us to understand rather than to criticize, to lean into acceptance rather than punish, and it allows for a balanced, mindful approach to life. If we can learn from compassion, it can create bridges between us, drawing us closer together so we can see that we are all able to feel pain. Although we don't always agree, we can at least find some overlap within which to collaborate and do business together, even if that is the business of affording respect to the other person. We have evolved to cooperate with each other, and collaboration is essential because we cannot avoid people, no matter how hard we try. We need medical help from others, we need to do business with each other, we need to learn, and we need to feel a sense of community and belonging. As there is no way to avoid collaboration, I'm always confused when people seem unwilling to learn how to do it more effectively. People still seem to think that they can remain intact, confined to their own little world, as if reality is not about to burst that bubble with the next turn of events.

When people struggle to buy into the concept of compassion, and the benefits of wider society seem too intangible, I try to help them understand the positive psychological benefits, such as a release of oxytocin, the calming hormone that is released during sex and play. Research shows that greater amounts of compassion result in less "self-criticism, depression, anxiety, rumination, thought suppression, and neurotic perfectionism." It also contributes to a greater sense of "life satisfaction and social connectedness," as reported in "Self-Compassion And Reactions To Unpleasant Self-Relevant Events: The Implications Of Treating Oneself Kindly." As clinical psychologist Paul Gilbert explains in *The Compassionate Mind: A New Approach to Life's Challenges*, compassion is an essential component to a balanced emotional state. We switch between one of three different systems to manage our emotions, and this includes our drive system (to achieve goals, for example), our threat system (to survive or seek safety, for example), and our soothing system (for compassion, or to soothe others, for example). We need a balance of all three systems, and without that, our ability to regulate our emotions, and ultimately our mental health, suffers. Gilbert explains that "caring and being helpful to others are seen as the most important personal motives and values, offering sources of meaning and pleasure in one's life. Conversely, the feeling that we have nothing to contribute and that we are 'not needed by anyone' can be a source of depression."

According to Gilbert, writing in "The Origins and Nature of Compassion Focused Therapy," "the most pervasive problems in mental health are for people who struggle to build affiliative relationships and experience isolation; people who have little interest in the well-being of others and are exploitative and harmful to others, and of course people who treat themselves in pretty hostile, uncaring, and non-compassionate ways." In other words, the more we remain within the confines of our Internal Prison, or the External Prison of structural inequality and privilege, the greater damage we will inflict on our mental health.

To truly reach beyond our confines, we need compassion, and we need to search for that middle ground, that small corner of overlap. You don't have to love someone to experience peace—you don't even have to like them—but you do need to connect with others, a moment of reciprocity where you can both feel like the other has met at least one need. A moment when you understand that there is no prison, no wall to divide *us* from *them*, and we are one.

CONCLUSION

Confinement can sometimes work. You need to give yourself room to breathe, space to grow, and a safe or calm place to gather yourself. You need a chance to activate the ventral vagal response of your parasympathetic nervous system, so you can connect and heal, and you need to give yourself permission to rest within the confines of your natural inclination towards extroversion or introversion. When you confine yourself, you create a fire barrier to prevent burnout. When you confine yourself, you give yourself hope that you can break the cycle of adverse childhood experiences. When you confine yourself, you create a sense of certainty and safety. After all, aren't all our internal prisons constructed to make us feel safe, even if that safety is just an illusion? Our prisons give us certainty when we are hardwired to fear uncertainty, so it speaks to us at a visceral level. But to expect to safeguard ourselves against all uncertainty is as unrealistic as our hope for immortality (the ultimate form of uncertainty). Mental health is not about certainty, it is about awareness and balance. The walls of these prisons that we construct often block out the light of awareness that can help us see our way to equilibrium. When we claim to already *know*, in that blind-faith grasp for certainty, we do not learn or grow. We only see the white swans that others have told us about. We narrate stories to fill the gaps in our knowledge, often stories that create fable-like roles of the Hero or Rescuer, Victim, or Persecutor, and when we polarize in such a way, we create artificial barriers that make us believe that we have separated *them* from *us*—a concept as illusory as the separation of internal from the external.

To reach beyond your confines, the key to free your mind, requires an acknowledgement that there is no clear delineation between our internal and external worlds. After all, the very definition of the mind does not simply refer to the workings of a brain in a skull. As Dan Siegel explains in *The Developing Mind*, the mind is an "embodied and relational process that regulates the flow of energy and information." According to Siegel, "mental processes are a product of our inner neural connections as well as our interpersonal communicative connections with others." We are continuously in flux, affecting, and being affected by the environment in which we live, an environment we continuously create, and so there is no fixed place or destination of freedom in the form of autonomy or authenticity. It is a continual process that is interconnected with the environment, which affects us as much as we affect it. The more we can accept this interrelationship between us and our environment, the easier it is to see that there is no *them* and *us*, any more than there is an environment that is separate from us.

Too often we view environmental catastrophes as a spectacle to witness without acknowledging that our pollution is a form of slow-burn suicide. This lack of appreciation for interdependent relationships, and interconnected consequences, can also be seen in other devastating developments of late. We can see it in the Supreme Court decision to overturn Roe v Wade, the mass censorship and banning of books that inconveniently tell the truth about racism in the US, and we see it in the structural inequality that we are part of. None of this exists in a vacuum without influencing us and being influenced by us. As we are all interrelated, we all have a part to play in the resultant suffering, and so we can also all play a part in freeing each other from this pain. We cannot keep our eyes firmly shut to these prisons of our own creation; only wide-eyed awareness can help. We need to continuously develop awareness of our own process and how we create a prison for ourselves (and others) in the form of short-circuited thought patterns, emotion dysregulation, imprisoning messages from our past, our intolerance of uncertainty, and low self-esteem. We can now see that it is insufficient to refer to these as our Internal Prison because the dividing line between an Internal and External Prison is far from clear.

Take parenting. When we parent our children, we are influenced by, and we influence, them. We create an external world that is inevitably influenced by, and influences, our internal world. We also see the interconnectedness of cycles of adverse childhood experiences and how closely our inner child and actual children can interact. We like to believe that our past is somehow compartmentalized, but it inevitably influences our children, as much as it might impact our inner child.

To understand this, we just have to look at the evolving area of research called *epigenetics*. Siegel defines epigenesis as "the process in which experience alters the regulation of gene expression by way of changing the various molecules (histones and methyl groups) on the chromosome." Epigenetic research is rapidly evolving, and we are starting to learn how trauma can have a significant impact on the genes of the parent *and* their children. There is no way to separate or compartmentalize the harm this child and parent may experience—any more than it is possible to separate ourselves from the environmental pollution we are creating, any more than it is possible to separate ourselves from the structural inequality we perpetuate, any more than it is possible to delineate between an Internal and External Prison.

This epiphany delivers a chilling message of the potential harm we may knowingly and unknowingly cause to ourselves and others. It also offers a message of hope that it is *us*, not just some other person or organization, government, or nation, who can play an active part in alleviating this harm. We need to be increasingly aware of the imprisoning nature of polarized views, encroachment of boundaries, discrimination, and privilege. There is no greater prison that confines us than structural inequality and privilege, and this is not something *out there*, or affecting other people. We are integral to the imprisoning nature of it, but we are also integral to freedom from it. The keys to reach beyond these confines are within our grasp in the form of awareness of our own process, knowledge of concepts such as intersectional theory, empathy, compassion, collaboration, mindful awareness, and even the use of Polyvagal Theory to regulate our nervous system. Once we free ourselves from the stagnating prison of perpetual shutdown, fight-or-flight, or fawn responses, we can more fluidly use our *social engagement system* to connect with ourselves and others, and to heal, nurture and grow. We just need to be free to do this. Free from without, and free from within.

APPENDIX CRISIS

If you are in crisis, you must seek immediate, professional help.
Here are some of the ways you can seek help:

- Call 911 (if it is available in your area).
- Take yourself to the emergency room of your nearest hospital.
- Call a friend or family member and ask them to take you to the nearest emergency room.
- Call the National Suicide Helpline on 988 or https://988lifeline.org/

Know that when you are in crisis, your brain is less likely to function optimally. This means that you might only consider a limited list of options when there might be more ways to resolve the problems you are experiencing. For this reason, you should seek help so a trained professional can ensure your safety and help you get out of your current state of crisis.

NOTES

Introduction

Man's Search for Meaning, Viktor Frankl

Mindfulness for Beginners, Jon Kabat-Zinn

The Gift of Therapy, Irvin D. Yalom

Good Morning, Monster, Catherine Gildiner

Meditation is Not What You Think, Jon Kabat-Zinn

"Kincentric Ecology: Indigenous Perceptions of the Human Nature Relationship," Enrique Salmón
DOI:10.2307/2641288

The Polyvagal Theory, Stephen W. Porges

Chapter 1

Thus Spoke Zarathustra, Friedrich Nietzsche

"KFF COVID-19 Vaccine Monitor: Views on the Pandemic at Two Years," Grace Sparks, Liz Hamel, Ashley Kirzinger, Alex Montero and Mollyann Brodie
https://www.kff.org/coronavirus-covid-19/poll-finding/kff-covid-19-vaccine-monitor-pandemic-two-years/

"1918 Pandemic," Centers for Disease Control and Prevention https://www.cdc.gov/flu/pandemic-resources/1918-pandemic-h1n1.html

Pox Americana: The Great Smallpox Epidemic of 1775-82, Elizabeth Anne Fenn

"6 Lessons We Can Learn from Past Pandemics," Lisa Marshall https://www.colorado.edu/today/2020/04/08/6-lessons-we-can-learn-past-pandemics

"Codependency, Trauma and the Fawn Response," Peter Walker http://www.pete-walker.com/codependencyFawnResponse.htm

"Suicide Risk and Mental Disorders," Louise Bradvik https://www.ncbi.nlm.nih.gov/pmc/articles/PMC6165520/

The Developing Mind, Dan Siegel

Meditation is Not What You Think, Jon Kabat-Zinn

The Polyvagal Theory, Stephen W. Porges

The Polyvagal Theory in Therapy, Deb Dana

Posttraumatic Stress Disorder: The Victim's Guide to Healing & Recovery, Raymond B. Flannery Jr

"Toxic Stress," Harvard University https://developingchild.harvard.edu/science/key-concepts/toxic-stress/

Treating Complex Traumatic Stress Disorders in Adults, Christine A. Courtois and Julian D. Ford

Treatment of Complex Trauma, Christine A. Courtois and Julian D. Ford

Getting Past Your Past, Francine Shapiro

An EMDR Therapy Primer, Barbara J. Hensley

Trauma and Recovery, Judith Herman

Mindfulness for Beginners, Jon Kabat-Zinn

Waking The Tiger, Peter A. Levine

The Body Keeps the Score: Brain, Mind, and Body in the Healing of Trauma, Bessel A. van der Kolk

"Serve and Return," Harvard University https://developingchild.harvard.edu/science/key-concepts/serve-and-return/

"Lifelong Health," Harvard University https://developingchild.harvard.edu/science/deep-dives/lifelong-health/

Recovery: The Lost Art of Convalescence, Gavin Francis

Oxford Handbook of Anxiety and Related Disorders, Martin M. Antony and Murray B. Stein

"Commemorating Smallpox Eradication," World Health Organization https://www.who.int/news/item/08-05-2020-commemorating-smallpox-eradication-a-legacy-of-hope-for-covid-19-and-other-diseases

Human Nature and the Social Order, Charles Horton Cooley

Meditation is Not What You Think, Jon Kabat-Zinn

"The Compulsion to Repeat the Trauma: Re-Enactment, Revictimization, and Masochism," Bessel A. van der Kolk http://www.cirp.org/library/psych/vanderkolk/

"Brain Architecture," Harvard University https://developingchild.harvard.edu/science/key-concepts/brain-architecture/

"The Science of Adult Capabilities," Harvard University https://developingchild.harvard.edu/science/deep-dives/adult-capabilities/

Pox Americana: The Great Smallpox Epidemic of 1775-82, Elizabeth Anne Fenn

"6 Lessons We Can Learn from Past Pandemics," Lisa Marshall https://www.colorado.edu/today/2020/04/08/6-lessons-we-can-learn-past-pandemics

"Adult Neurogenesis in Humans – Common and Unique Traits in Mammals," Aurelie Ernst and Jonas Frisen doi:10.1371/journal.pbio.1002045

"Exercise Training Increases Size of Hippocampus and Improves Memory," Michelle W. Ross, Ruchika Shaurya Prakash and Arthur F. Kramer doi:10.1073/pnas.1015950108

"Human Hippocampal Neurogenesis Drops Sharply in Children to Undetectable Levels in Adults," Shawn F. Sorrells, Mercedes F. Paredes, Arantxa Cebrian-Silla et al, doi:10.1038/nature25975

Hamlet, William Shakespeare

The Feeling Good Handbook, David D. Burns

Neurosis and Human Growth: The Struggle Toward Self-Realization, Karen Horney

DBT Skills Training Manual, Marsha M. Linehan

Beyond the Blue, Chris Warren-Dickins

Chapter 2

Pox Americana: The Great Smallpox Epidemic of 1775-82, Elizabeth Anne Fenn

"6 Lessons We Can Learn from Past Pandemics," Lisa Marshall https://www.colorado.edu/today/2020/04/08/6-lessons-we-can-learn-past-pandemics

"Psychophysiological Characteristics of Burnout Syndrome: Resting-State EEG Analysis," Krystyna Golonka, Magda Gawlowska, Justyna Mojsa-Kaja and Tadeusz Marek doi: 10.1155/2019/3764354

"Understanding the Stress Response," Harvard University https://www.health.harvard.edu/staying-healthy/understanding-the-stress-response

"Burnout: Past, Present, and Future Concerns," Herbert J. Freudenberger https://www.tandfonline.com/doi/abs/10.1300/J132v03n01_01?journalCode=wzlg20

"Burn-Out An 'Occupational Phenomenon'", World Health Organization https://www.who.int/news/item/28-05-2019-burn-out-an-occupational-phenomenon-international-classification-of-diseases

"Burnout and Stress are Everywhere," American Psychological Association https://www.apa.org/monitor/2022/01/special-burnout-stress

Meditation is Not What You Think, Jon Kabat-Zinn

Recovery: The Lost Art of Convalescence, Gavin Francis

The Canterbury Tales, Geoffrey Chaucer

Quiet: The Power of Introverts in a World That Can't Stop Talking, Susan Cain

"Brief, Daily Meditation Enhances Attention, Memory, Mood, and Emotional Regulation in Non-Experienced Meditators," Julia C. Basso, Alexandra McHale, Victoria Ende, Douglas J. Oberlin, Wendy A. Suzuki sciencedirect.com/science/article/abs/pii/S016643281830322X

Full Catastrophe Living: Using the Wisdom of Your Body and Mind to Face Stress, Pain, and Illness, Jon Kabat-Zinn

"The Lost Art of Convalescence," The Wellcome Collection https://wellcomecollection.org/articles/XXurkhEAACgATLgi

"Brain Health Consequences of Digital Technology Use," Gary W. Small, Jooyeon Lee, Aaron Kaufman, Jason Jalil, Prabha Siddarth, et al https://www.ncbi.nlm.nih.gov/pmc/articles/PMC7366948/

Psychological Types, Carl Jung

Beyond the Blue, Chris Warren-Dickins

Chapter 3

"Computations of Uncertainty Mediate Acute Stress Responses in Humans," Archy O. de Berker, Robb B. Rutledge, Christoph Mathys, Louise Marshall, Gemma F. Cross, et al https://www.nature.com/articles/ncomms10996

"The Implications of COVID-19 for Mental Health and Substance Use," Nirmita Panchal, Rabah Kamah, Cynthia Cox and Rachael Garfield https://www.kff.org/coronavirus-covid-19/issue-brief/the-implications-of-covid-19-for-mental-health-and-substance-use/

"The Origins and Nature of Compassion Focused Therapy," Paul Gilbert - https://self-compassion.org/wp-content/uploads/publications/GilbertCFT.pdf

The Polyvagal Theory, Stephen W. Porges

The New Science of Breath, Stephen Elliott and Dee Edmonson

The Polyvagal Theory in Therapy, Deb Dana

The Black Swan, The Impact of the Highly Improbable, Nassim Nicholas Taleb

The Collected Novels and Memoirs of William Godwin Vol 8, Volume 8, Pamela Clemit, Maurice Hindle, Mark Philp

The Gift of Therapy, Irvin D. Yalom

"Fairy Tales and Script Drama Analysis," Stephen B. Karpman https://karpmandramatriangle.com/pdf/DramaTriangle.pdf

The Confidence Game, Maria Konnikova

"5 Questions for Arie W. Kruglanski," American Psychological Association https://www.apa.org/monitor/2019/04/conversation-kruglanski

"United Nations Handbook on Children Recruited and Exploited by Terrorist and Violent Extremist Groups," United Nations Office on Drugs and Crime https://www.unodc.org/documents/justice-and-prison-reform/Child-Victims/Handbook_on_Children_Recruited_and_Exploited_by_Terrorist_and_Violent_Extremist_Groups_the_Role_of_the_Justice_System.E.pdf

The Roots of Evil: The Psychological and Cultural Origins of Genocide and Other Forms of Group Violence, Ervin Staub

"From Uncertainty to Extremism," Michael A. Hogg https://sites.bu.edu/marshfellows/files/2021/05/0963721414540168.pdf

When the Body Says No: The Cost of Hidden Stress, Gabor Maté

"What Really Matters at the End of Life," BJ Miller https://www.ted.com/talks/bj_miller_what_really_matters_at_the_end_of_life?language=en

Beyond the Blue, Chris Warren-Dickins

Chapter 4

"The Implications of COVID-19 for Mental Health and Substance Use," Nirmita Panchal, Rabah Kamah, Cynthia Cox and Rachael Garfield https://www.kff.org/coronavirus-covid-19/issue-brief/the-implications-of-covid-19-for-mental-health-and-substance-use/

The Problem of Pain, C.S. Lewis

"Suicide Risk and Mental Disorders," Louise Bradvik https://www.ncbi.nlm.nih.gov/pmc/articles/PMC6165520/

The Polyvagal Theory, Stephen W. Porges

The Bell Jar, Sylvia Plath

Crisis Intervention: A Handbook of Immediate Person-to-Person Help, Kenneth France

Huckleberry Finn, Mark Twain

Narrative Approaches to Working with Adult Male Survivors, Kim Etherington

I'm a Joke and So Are You: Reflections on Humour and Humanity, Robin Ince

"The Imposter Phenomenon in High Achieving Women: Dynamics and Therapeutic Intervention," Suzanne Imes and Rose Clance https://psycnet.apa.org/doiLanding?doi=10.1037%2Fh0086006

DBT Skills Training Manual, Marsha M. Linehan

Chapter 5

The Polyvagal Theory, Stephen W. Porges

The Polyvagal Theory in Therapy, Deb Dana

"The Implications of COVID-19 for Mental Health and Substance Use," Nirmita Panchal, Rabah Kamah, Cynthia Cox and Rachael Garfield https://www.kff.org/coronavirus-covid-19/issue-brief/the-implications-of-covid-19-for-mental-health-and-substance-use/

"KFF COVID-19 Vaccine Monitor: Views on the Pandemic at Two Years," Grace Sparks, Liz Hamel, Ashley Kirzinger, Alex Montero and Mollyann Brodie https://www.kff.org/coronavirus-covid-19/poll-finding/kff-covid-19-vaccine-monitor-pandemic-two-years/

"Worlds of Influence – Understanding What Shapes Child Well-being in Rich Countries - Report Card 16," UNICEF https://www.unicef-irc.org/publications/pdf/Report-Card-16-Worlds-of-Influence-child-wellbeing.pdf

"Launch of the UNICEF Report Card 17," UNICEF https://www.outdoorplaycanada.ca/2022/04/29/launch-of-the-unicef-report-card-17-and-echo-events/

Trauma and Recovery, Judith Herman

The Body Keeps the Score, Bessel A. van der Kolk

"Toxic Stress," Harvard University https://developingchild.harvard.edu/science/key-concepts/toxic-stress/

DBT Skills Training Manual, Marsha M. Linehan

Permission to Feel: Unlocking the Power of Emotions to Help Our Kids, Ourselves and Our Society Thrive, Marc Brackett

Full Catastrophe Living: Using The Wisdom of Your Body and Mind to Face Stress, Pain, and Illness, Jon Kabat-Zinn

The New Science of Breath, Stephen Elliott and Dee Edmonson

Playing and Reality, D. W. Winnicott

The Child, the Family, and the Outside World, D. W. Winnicott

A Good Enough Parent, Bruno Bettelheim

Beyond the Blue, Chris Warren-Dickins

"Annual TikTok User Growth In The United States from 2019 to 2024," Statista https://www.statista.com/statistics/1100842/tiktok-us-user-growth/#:~:text=In%202020%2C%20TikTok%20increased%20it's,users%20in%20the%20United%20States.

"Brain Health Consequences of Digital Technology Use," Gary W. Small, Jooyeon Lee, Aaron Kaufman, Jason Jalil, Prabha Siddarth, et al https://www.ncbi.nlm.nih.gov/pmc/articles/PMC7366948/

"Parenting Approaches And Concerns Related To Digital Devices," Pew Research Center https://www.pewresearch.org/internet/2020/07/28/parenting-approaches-and-concerns-related-to-digital-devices/

Chapter 6

Politics 5, Aristotle, translated by Benjamin Jowett

"The Cost of Coming Out," Lesley University https://lesley.edu/article/the-cost-of-coming-out-lgbt-youth-homelessness

"About True Colors United," True Colors United https://truecolorsunited.org/about/

"Working With Homeless LGBTQ Youth," Lambda Legal https://www.lambdalegal.org/know-your-rights/article/youth-homeless

"Third of British LGBTQ+ People Experience Abuse by Relatives," Libby Brooks https://www.theguardian.com/world/2022/apr/01/third-of-young-british-lgbtq-people-experience-abuse-by-relatives

"Intersection of Trauma and Identity," Edward Alessi and James Martin https://socialwork.rutgers.edu/sites/default/files/alessi-martin2017_chapter_intersectionoftraumaandidentit.pdf

"Discussing Discrimination," American Psychological Association https://www.apa.org/topics/racism-bias-discrimination/keita

"Like Walking Through a Hailstorm," Human Rights Watch https://www.hrw.org/report/2016/12/08/walking-through-hailstorm/discrimination-against-lgbt-youth-us-schools#

Treating Complex Traumatic Stress Disorders in Adults, Christine A. Courtois and Julian D. Ford

Treatment of Complex Trauma, Christine A. Courtois and Julian D. Ford

Human Nature and the Social Order, Charles Horton Cooley

"A Year After Charlottesville, Not Much Has Changed For Trump," Ayesha Rascoe https://www.npr.org/2018/08/11/637665414/a-year-after-charlottesville-not-much-has-changed-for-trump

American Counseling Association https://www.counseling.org/resources/aca-code-of-ethics.pdf

A Theory of Cognitive Dissonance, Leon Festinger

"Why Facts Don't Change Our Minds," Elizabeth Kolbert https://www.newyorker.com/magazine/2017/02/27/why-facts-dont-change-our-minds

The Confidence Game, Maria Konnikova

The Knowledge Illusion: Why We Never Think Alone, Steven Sloman and Philip Fernbach

Dying for Ideas: The Dangerous Lives of the Philosophers, Costica Bradatan

"Documents Reveal Facebook Targeted Children As Young As 6 For Consumer Base," Ezra Kaplan and Jo Ling Kent https://www.nbcnews.com/tech/social-media/facebook-documents-reveal-company-targeted-children-young-6-rcna4021

Witches: Evolving Perceptions, Rachel Christ-Doane

Malleus Maleficarum, Heinrich Kramer

"Women Of Color Will Lose the Most if Roe v Wade is Overturned," Jamila Taylor https://www.americanprogress.org/article/women-color-will-lose-roe-v-wade-overturned/

A Modern Introduction to the Family, Ezra F. Vogel and Norman W. Bell

The Nature of Human Prejudice, Gordon W. Allport

Collected Works of C. G. Jung, Vol. 16. 2nd ed., Princeton University Press

"National Report (Through December 31, 2021)," Stop AAPI Hate https://stopaapihate.org/national-report-through-december-31-2021/

Pox Americana: The Great Smallpox Epidemic of 1775-82, Elizabeth Anne Fenn

"6 Lessons We Can Learn from Past Pandemics," Lisa Marshall https://www.colorado.edu/today/2020/04/08/6-lessons-we-can-learn-past-pandemics

"The Necessary and Sufficient Conditions of Therapeutic Personality Change," Carl Rogers

Toward Effective Counseling and Psychotherapy, Charles B. Truax and Robert R.Carkhuff

"A Method of Self-Evaluation for Counselor Education Utilizing the Measurement of Facilitative Condition," Donald

G. Martin and George M. Gazda
https://onlinelibrary.wiley.com/doi/10.1002/j.1556-6978.1970.tb01368.x

Intentional Interviewing and Counseling, Allen E. Ivey, Mary Bradford Ivey and Carlos P. Zalaquett

Paul Bloom
https://www.theatlantic.com/health/archive/2015/10/a-short-history-of-empathy/409912/

Chapter 7

Meditation Is Not What You Think, Jon Kabat-Zinn

"The Brain In Solitude: An (Other) Eighth Amendment Challenge to Solitary Confinement," Federica Coppola
https://academic.oup.com/jlb/article/6/1/184/5573653

The Art of Happiness, HH Dalai Lama and Howard C. Cutler

Set Boundaries, Find Peace, Nedra Glover Tawwab

The Four Agreements: A Practical Guide to Personal Freedom, Don Miguel Ruiz

Stop Walking on Eggshells, Paul Mason and Randi Kreger

National Domestic Violence Hotline https://www.thehotline.org/ or 1-800-799-SAFE

Child Welfare Information Gateway
https://www.childwelfare.gov/

The Emotionally Abusive Relationship: How To Stop Being Abused And How To Stop Abusing, Beverly Engel

"Emotional Abuse in Intimate Relationships: The Role of Gender and Age," Gunnur Karakurt and Kristin E. Silver https://www.ncbi.nlm.nih.gov/pmc/articles/PMC3876290/

"Adverse Childhood Experiences and Health in Adulthood in a Rural Population-Based Sample," Kristen C. Iniguez and Rachel V. Stankowski https://www.ncbi.nlm.nih.gov/pmc/articles/PMC5302459/

"The Health and Social Consequences of Adverse Childhood Experiences (ACE) Across the Lifespan: An Introduction to Prevention and Intervention in the Community," Heather Larkin, Joseph J. Shields, Robert F Anda https://pubmed.ncbi.nlm.nih.gov/22970779/

American Association of University Women https://www.aauw.org/resources/research/crossing-the-line-sexual-harassment-at-school/

"Crossing the Line: Sexual Harassment at School," Catherine Hill and Holly Kearl https://www.aauw.org/app/uploads/2020/03/Crossing-the-Line-Sexual-Harassment-at-School.pdf

"Sexual Harassment Common among Middle School Children, Study Finds," University of Illinois at Urbana-Champaign https://www.sciencedaily.com/releases/2016/12/161209184825.htm

"The Disturbing Connection Between Bullying and Sexual Harassment," Dorothy Espelage https://theconversation.com/the-disturbing-connection-between-bullying-and-sexual-harassment-68033

"Who We Are," Stop Sexual Assault in Schools https://stopsexualassaultinschools.org/who-we-are/

"Know Your Rights," Stop Sexual Assault in Schools https://stopsexualassaultinschools.org/know-your-rights/

"Checklist for a Comprehensive Approach to Addressing Harassment," Department of Education https://www2.ed.gov/about/offices/list/ocr/checklist.html

Chapter 8

Jane Eyre, Charlotte Bronte

Childhood and Society, Erik Erikson

The Life Cycle Completed, Erik Erikson

Treating Complex Traumatic Stress Disorders in Adults, Christine A. Courtois and Julian D. Ford

Treatment of Complex Trauma, Christine A. Courtois and Julian D. Ford

Trauma and Recovery, Judith Herman

"Assessing Challenges, Needs, and Innovations of Gender-Based Violence Services during the COVID-19 Pandemic: Results Summary Report," University of Texas at San Antonio, College for Health, Community and Policy, National Coalition Against Domestic Violence (NCADV), Kellie Lynch and TK Logan https://assets.speakcdn.com/assets/2497/covid__gender_based_violence_final_report.pdf).

"Devastatingly Pervasive: 1 in 3 Women Globally Experience Violence," World Health Organization https://www.who.int/news/item/09-03-2021-devastatingly-pervasive-1-in-3-women-globally-experience-violence

"Measuring the Shadow Pandemic: Violence against Women During COVID-19," United Nations https://data.unwomen.org/publications/vaw-rga

The Body Keeps the Score: Brain, Mind, and Body in the Healing of Trauma, Bessel A. van der Kolk

"The Compulsion to Repeat the Trauma: Re-Enactment, Revictimization, and Masochism," Bessel A. van der Kolk http://www.cirp.org/library/psych/vanderkolk/

Waking The Tiger, Peter A. Levine

"The Stockholm Syndrome. On the Psychological Reaction of Hostages and Hostage-Takers," R Harnischmacher and J Müther https://pubmed.ncbi.nlm.nih.gov/3662732/

"Stockholm Syndrome: Held Hostage by the One You Love," Matthew H. Logan https://www.liebertpub.com/doi/10.1089/vio.2017.0076

"Reflections on the Patty Hearst case," B J Montgomery https://pubmed.ncbi.nlm.nih.gov/448874/

"Terry Anderson, Terry Waite, and Thomas Sutherland kidnapping," Syracuse University http://law.syr.edu/uploads/docs/academics/ARTICLE_2_Attached_to_Pander_Report.pdf

"Kidnapping and Hostage-Taking: A Review of Effects, Coping and Resilience," David A Alexander and Susan Klein https://www.ncbi.nlm.nih.gov/pmc/articles/PMC2627800/

"'Stockholm Syndrome': Psychiatric Diagnosis Or Urban Myth?," M. Namnyak, N. Tufton, R. Szekely, M. Toal, S Worboys, E.L. Sampson https://www.researchgate.net/publication/5819575_'Stockholm_syndrome'_Psychiatric_diagnosis_or_urban_myth/link/5a62167b4585158bca4aae52/download

"A Socioanalytic Theory of Moral Development," R Hogan, J. A. Johnson, N. P. Emler Doi:10.1002/cd.23219780203

Games People Play, Eric Berne

Beyond the Blue, Chris Warren-Dickins

"Empirical Foundations for Writing in Prevention and Psychotherapy: Mental and Physical Health Outcomes," B. A. Esterling, L. L'Abate, E. J. Murray, and J. W. Pennebaker https://pubmed.ncbi.nlm.nih.gov/9987585/

Understanding Narrative Therapy: A Guidebook for the Social Worker, P. Abels, S. Abels

Full Catastrophe Living: Using the Wisdom of Your Body and Mind to Face Stress, Pain, And Illness, Jon Kabat-Zinn

"The Benefits of Being Present: Mindfulness and its Role in Psychological Well-Being," Kirk Warren Brown and Richard M. Ryan https://selfdeterminationtheory.org/SDT/documents/2003_BrownRyan.pdf

"2014 ACA Code of Ethics," American Counseling Association https://www.counseling.org/resources/aca-code-of-ethics.pdf

Crisis Intervention: A Handbook of Immediate Person-to-Person Help, Kenneth France

"The Porosity of Autonomy: Social and Biological Constitution of the Patient in Biomedicine," Jonathan Beever and Nicolae Morar https://philarchive.org/archive/BEETPO-8

"Biological Autonomy," A. Grandpierre and Menas Kafatos https://digitalcommons.chapman.edu/cgi/viewcontent.cgi?article=1171&context=scs_articles

"Kincentric Ecology: Indigenous Perceptions of the Human Nature Relationship," Enrique Salmón DOI:10.2307/2641288

Adventures in Being Human, Gavin Francis

Chapter 9

"Authenticity," Stanford University https://plato.stanford.edu/entries/authenticity/

"Toward a Social Psychology of Authenticity: Exploring Within-Person Variation in Autonomy, Congruence, and Genuineness Using Self-Determination Theory," William S. Ryan, Richard M. Ryan https://doi.org/10.1037/gpr0000162

Meditation Is Not What You Think, Jon Kabat-Zinn

The Power of Now, Eckhart Tolle

On Being Authentic, Charles Guignon

Existential Therapy and Psychotherapeutic Practice, H. W. Cohn

Everyday Mysteries: Existential Dimensions of Psychotherapy, Emmy van Deurzen-Smith

A Year to Live, Stephen Levine

Spiritual Verses: The First Book of the Masnavi-ye Ma'navi, The Jalaluddin Rumi

Full Catastrophe Living: Using the Wisdom of Your Body and Mind to Face Stress, Pain, and Illness, Jon Kabat-Zinn

"The Mindful Self: A Mindfulness-Enlightened Self-View," Qianguo Xiao, Caizhen Yue, Weijie He, and Jia-yuan Yu https://www.ncbi.nlm.nih.gov/pmc/articles/PMC5645519/

Mindfulness for Beginners, Jon Kabat-Zinn

Focusing, Eugene Gendlin

"How to Quit Your Job in the Great Post-Pandemic Resignation Boom," Bloomberg https://www.bloomberg.com/news/articles/2021-05-10/quit-your-job-how-to-resign-after-covid-pandemic

US Bureau of Labor Statistics https://www.bls.gov/news.release/archives/jolts_10122021.htm

"The Psychologist Who Coined the Phrase 'Great Resignation,'" Juliana Kaplan https://www.businessinsider.com/why-everyone-is-quitting-great-resignation-psychologist-pandemic-rethink-life-2021-10

Kierkegaard's Philosophy: Self-deception and Cowardice in the Present Age, J. D. Mullen

Chapter 10

"The Black Cholera Comes to the Central Valley of America in the 19th Century - 1832, 1849, and Later," Walter J. Daly https://www.ncbi.nlm.nih.gov/pmc/articles/PMC2394684/

Pox Americana: The Great Smallpox Epidemic of 1775-82, Elizabeth Anne Fenn

"'It's Scary': Gay Men Confront a Health Crisis With Echoes of the Past," New York Times https://www.nytimes.com/2022/07/28/nyregion/gay-men-monkeypox-health-crisis.html

"As Monkeypox Spreads, Know The Difference Between Warning and Stigmatizing People," NPR https://www.npr.org/2022/07/26/1113713684/monkeypox-stigma-gay-community

"6 Lessons We Can Learn From Past Pandemics," Lisa Marshall https://www.colorado.edu/today/2020/04/08/6-lessons-we-can-learn-past-pandemics

"National Report (Through December 31, 2021)," Stop AAPI Hate https://stopaapihate.org/national-report-through-december-31-2021/

"Structural Racism and Inequalities in Health," Taylor W. Hargrove https://www.asanet.org/news-events/footnotes/apr-may-jun-2021/features/structural-racism-and-inequalities-health

“Structural Inequality: The Real COVID-19 Threat to America’s Health and How Strengthening the Affordable Care Act Can Help,” Dayna Bowen Matthew https://www.law.georgetown.edu/georgetown-law-journal/wp-content/uploads/sites/26/2020/06/Matthew_Structural-Inequality-The-Real-COVID-19-Threat-to-America%E2%80%99s-Health-and-How-Strengthening-the-Affordable-Care-Act-Can-Help.pdf

“The Implications of COVID-19 for Mental Health and Substance Use,” Nirmita Panchal, Rabah Kamah, Cynthia Cox and Rachael Garfield https://www.kff.org/coronavirus-covid-19/issue-brief/the-implications-of-covid-19-for-mental-health-and-substance-use/

“Women of Color Will Lose the Most if Roe v Wade is Overturned,” Jamila Taylor https://www.americanprogress.org/article/women-color-will-lose-roe-v-wade-overturned/

“Demarginalizing the Intersection of Race and Sex: A Black Feminist Critique of Antidiscrimination Doctrine, Feminist Theory and Antiracist Politics,” Kimberlé Crenshaw https://chicagounbound.uchicago.edu/cgi/viewcontent.cgi?article=1052&context=uclf

"What is Intersectionality and Why is it Important?”, Anne Sisson Runyan https://www.aaup.org/article/what-intersectionality-and-why-it-important#.YmBJlvPMJQ1

"2014 ACA Code of Ethics," American Counseling Association https://www.counseling.org/resources/aca-code-of-ethics.pdf

"The Weirdest People in the World?" Joe Henrich, Steven J. Heine and Ara Norenzayan, https://papers.ssrn.com/sol3/papers.cfm?abstract_id=1601785

"Too Early to Tell: The Potential Impact and Challenges—Ethical and Otherwise—Inherent in the Mainstreaming of Dharma in an Increasingly Dystopian World," Jon Kabat-Zinn https://link.springer.com/article/10.1007/s12671-017-0758-2

"Kincentric Ecology: Indigenous Perceptions of the Human Nature Relationship," Enrique Salmón DOI:10.2307/2641288

Call Us What We Carry, Amanda Gorman

"Why Facts Don't Change Our Minds," Elizabeth Kolbert https://www.newyorker.com/magazine/2017/02/27/why-facts-dont-change-our-minds

"Empathy Toward Strangers Triggers Oxytocin Release and Subsequent Generosity,"
Jorge A Barraza and Paul J Zak
https://pubmed.ncbi.nlm.nih.gov/19580564/

"The Orgasmic History of Oxytocin: Love, Lust, and Labor,"
Navneet Magon and Sanjay Kalra
https://www.ncbi.nlm.nih.gov/pmc/articles/PMC3183515/

"Self-Compassion and Reactions To Unpleasant Self-Relevant Events: The Implications of Treating Oneself

Kindly," Mark R. Leary, Eleanor B. Tate, Claire E. Adams, Ashley Batts Allen and Jessica Hancock doi:10.1037/0022-3514.92.5.887

"An Examination of Self-Compassion in Relation to Positive Psychological Functioning and Personality Traits," K.D. Neff, S. S. Rude and K. Kirkpatrick doi:10.1016/j.jrp.2006.08.002

The Compassionate Mind: A New Approach to Life's Challenges, Paul Gilbert

"The Origins and Nature of Compassion Focused Therapy," Paul Gilbert https://self-compassion.org/wp-content/uploads/publications/GilbertCFT.pdf

Conclusion

The Developing Mind, Dan Siegel

"Intergenerational Transmission of Trauma Effects: Putative Role of Epigenetic Mechanisms," Rachel Yehuda and Amy Lehrner https://www.ncbi.nlm.nih.gov/pmc/articles/PMC6127768/

The Polyvagal Theory, Stephen W. Porges

ABOUT THE AUTHOR

Figure - Chris Warren-Dickins LLB MA LPC.
Photo credit: Jean Terman Photography

Chris Warren-Dickins is a psychotherapist and author of *Beyond the Blue*. They provide a psychotherapy service that serves people in New Jersey (USA) and the United Kingdom. Chris loves to help all sorts of people with all sorts of problems, and they tend to work on the following areas: Eye movement desensitization and reprocessing therapy (EMDR) (an approach commonly used for trauma), Affirmative LGBTQ+ therapy, and "Men's therapy" (in other words, how to survive the male label).

Chris was educated at University College London and University of East London (United Kingdom), and in 2010 Chris was awarded a masters in counseling and psychotherapy. This included qualitative research into male-labeled experiences of suicide and counseling.

Before qualifying as a psychotherapist, Chris was a senior lawyer in London, but realized that they enjoyed helping people feel safe more than acquiring sites for redevelopment.

After building a successful psychotherapy practice in London, Chris moved to the United States, to enable their two children to see more of their American grandparents, cousins, and extended family. Since 2018, Chris has been running a private psychotherapy practice in Ridgewood, New Jersey as a Licensed Professional Counselor (LPC).

Chris would love it if you reached out and made contact.
Please do so via the Contact page at
www.chriswarrendickins.com.

OTHER BOOKS

BY CHRIS WARREN-DICKINS LLB MA LPC

Beyond the Blue: A Survival Guide for the Male Labeled, and a Healthier Society for All
By Chris Warren-Dickins LLB MA LPC

Does any of this sound familiar?

- Depression snarls at you like a beast.
- Anxiety burns through the pit of your stomach like a fireball.
- You are constantly angry and in conflict with people around you.
- A ten-ton trauma drags you down.

Without the right help, any one of these issues can threaten your career, your business, or your personal relationships.

What if you discovered that you already carry survival tools to help you to tackle these threats to your emotional and physical well-being?

Like blazes on a trail, this Survival Guide will guide you through the rougher paths of the journey that is your life, teaching you how to prepare for these darker days, what to do when the storm arrives, and how to survive and thrive so you do not plunge from disturbance to crisis. Within these pages, you will find advice that is based on the latest research in neuroscience, strategies from the most effective approaches to psychotherapy, and Chris Warren-Dickins's experience as a psychotherapist.

This Survival Guide offers an alternative approach to the corner-cutting logic that is labeling. When it comes to surviving depression, anxiety, relationship conflict, or trauma, labels can sometimes fail to help because we are more complex and sophisticated than that.

Chris invites us to look beyond the blue of the male label that was given to us with an appreciation that our lived reality may differ compared with some of the assumptions associated with this label. These assumptions are significant obstacles to adequate mental health care, and the reality is that there is little opportunity for adequate and accessible mental health care for people who have been given the male label. This was already a problem before the pandemic, and now it has become a healthcare crisis. Untreated depression, anxiety, relationship conflict, and trauma pose a risk for all of us in society.

This Survival Guide offers adequate and accessible mental health care so you can survive and thrive despite depression, anxiety, relationship conflict, and trauma. If you are still in need of help beyond this book, there is advice about how to separate the good from the bad and ugly forms of professional help.

Are you ready to take your next step *Beyond the Blue*?

***

Praise for *Beyond the Blue*, by Chris Warren-Dickins LLB MA LPC

"Beyond the Blue *is a thoughtful pathway to healthy living. Chris well understands that modern life is difficult and offers sound research from neuroscience, psychotherapy, and his professional experience.* Beyond the Blue *is accessible, 'achievable' and sensible, and well researched. It's a welcome reference for any and every person who is 'male labeled.'*"
- The Honorable James E. McGreevey. Governor of New Jersey 2002 – 2004

"*Stigma, societal beliefs, label-based expectations, and no clear road map to care are real and pressing issues.* Beyond the Blue *peels back these obstacles and provides a user friendly 'survival guide' to self-care in a complicated world and meaningful clinical advice about seeking professional care. Don't just survive, choose to thrive.* Beyond the Blue *can help with that journey.*"

- David J. Griffith, MS, CCS, LCADC. President & C.E.O. | Vantage Health System

"Beyond the Blue *is packed with tools to 'survive and thrive.' Chris Warren-Dickins provides essential psychoeducation accompanied by awareness and solution-based exercises that are sure to benefit any willing reader. The author's personal passion to offer help to the male labeled is unquestionable."*
- Jill Fellner, MSW, LCSW

"Chris Warren-Dickins's survival guide is not only for the male labeled but is also a resource for anyone challenged by abuse, anxiety, and depression. Packed with fresh new metaphors and time-tested exercises, this book speaks knowingly to a whole spectrum of human experiences and identities. Beyond the Blue *is a timely addition to self-help and professional references."*
- Suzanne Saldarini, MA, LPC, NCPsyA

***

For more information - www.chriswarrendickins.com

INDEX

F

G

H

I

K

L

M

N

O

P

R

S

CPSIA information can be obtained
at www.ICGtesting.com
Printed in the USA
LVHW081620171122
733197LV00012B/284

9 798985 102420